THE ANONYMOUS CHRISTIAN

THE
Anonymous Christian
by Anita Röper

translated by Joseph Donceel, S.J.

WITH AN AFTERWORD
The Anonymous Christian According to Karl Rahner
by Klaus Riesenhuber, S.J.

SHEED AND WARD : NEW YORK

© Sheed and Ward, Inc., 1966

Translated from Die Anonymen Christen by
Anita Röper © 1963 by Matthias-Grünewald-Verlag Mainz.

Afterword: "The Anonymous Christian According to Karl Rahner"
by Klaus Riesenhuber, S.J., translated with the permission of
Verlag Herder Wien from the Article "Der Anonyme Christ nach
Karl Rahner" in Zeitschrift für katholische Theologie, 86 (1964).

Library of Congress Catalog Card Number: 66–12269

Manufactured in the United States of America

Preface

Has the Redemption failed? Has the Word of God come to earth and suffered and died in vain? The question might well be raised, when we look around us on earth and note the relatively small number of Christians. All salvation is of Christ and through Christ, and there are hundreds of millions of people who have never heard of him, or, having heard of him, consider him only as one great man among so many others.

In this remarkable book Anita Röper tries to show that reality far surpasses the appearances. The number of Christians on our twentieth-century earth seems pitifully small only if we overlook the countless millions of "anonymous Christians" who live among us, as they live among Moslems and Hindus, in pagan countries and behind the Iron Curtain. These are the people who may never have heard of Christ, or have a very vague or wholly distorted knowledge of him, and who, nevertheless, have met and welcomed his loving invitation in the hidden depths of their heart. These are the countless millions of humble people who, all over the earth, live according to their lights, these are the "men of good will."

We know and profess that God wishes all men to be saved and to come into possession of the truth. The Church has always firmly upheld the doctrine of the universal salvific will of God. On the other hand, she states as constantly (though not in the sense that Church membership need be either jurid- ical or even perceived) that "outside the Church there is no salvation." She must state this, since all salvation comes through Christ, and man meets Christ only in and through the Church.

It is not too difficult to understand how a man of good will may eventually meet God and love him. For what is man ultimately but an embodied affirmation of the Absolute? Anita Röper explains this lucidly in her book. But man is not saved by the Absolute, but by Christ. Can a man of good will, who has never heard of him, who may never come to hear of him, ever meet him and follow him into his Church?

Karl Rahner believes he can, and in various parts of his works has hinted at a possible solution of this vital problem. Frau Röper wholly agrees with him. She has assimilated and she deftly uses the scattered hints of the great theologian. She mentions him only once, briefly, in her short foreword, but her book is in fact an original, clear and persuasive presenta- tion of some of the most profound themes of his theology.

The thought of Karl Rahner is admittedly not always easy to follow and to grasp. To make sure that Anita Röper really had understood him, the best thing was to consult him. I received the following reply to my inquiry, which Father Rahner kindly allows me to quote:

I wholeheartedly approve your plan of translating the book. I had already read the German manuscript of Anita Röper's book, and advised the author while she was writing it. It is *her* book. And of course I would have said many things in a slightly different way if I had been writing the book myself. But it is a good book. And you do well by translating it. The book has just been translated into Dutch. A French translation will come out too, and probably also a Spanish one. This is an important topic. By all means translate the book.

I would like you also to consider the following suggestion, although you and your publishers remain, of course, wholly free. The *Zeitschrift für katholische Theologie* has published a short paper by Kl. Riesenhuber, S.J., on "the anonymous Christian according to Karl Rahner." Might it not be possible to translate this short paper and add it to the Röper book as an appendix? This would supply the reader with theological precisions and bibliographical data which would enhance the value of the work.

Father Rahner's suggestions seemed excellent, and the reader will find, as an Afterword to this book, a translation of the article by Father Riesenhuber, with precise references to the translated and the as yet untranslated writings of Rahner on the topic so masterfully treated by Frau Röper in this bold exploratory work, which opens up new areas of theological speculation concerning a subject on which the final word has not been said.

J. DONCEEL, S.J.

Author's Note

Concerning the topic treated in this book Karl Rahner has already said many things, although only by way of hints and in a way which only professional theologians can understand. Yet the topic is so important that it should also be developed once in a way suitable for a wider circle of readers. It is, of course, unavoidable that many ideas and themes which are to be found in Rahner will be taken over and used in this work. Nevertheless, only the author is responsible for the way in which the matter is here presented.

Contents

Contents

1/ The Situation

Almost two thousand years have elapsed since Christ told his Apostles: "Go ye and teach all nations!" True, two thousand years do not mean much in the long history of mankind. Nevertheless some results might be expected from the fulfillment of that mission. How has it been fulfilled? Christianity is but a small segment within the history of humanity. It has not managed to strike solid roots in any of the major civilizations other than the culture of its own origin. It has entered into symbiosis only with the Greco-Roman civilization. But China? Japan? or India? It ought to be possible for a Chinese to be a Chinese *and* a Christian, for a Japanese to be a Japanese and a Christian exactly as a Greco-Roman, Western man may be at the same time a Greco-Roman Westerner and a Christian. Yet, apart from insignificant minorities, this is not the case, and these minorities, by remaining minorities, confirm the rule. It is important to remember that the roots of Christianity in the Old Testament are very widespreading, reaching into Assyria, Babylonia, Egypt and Persia, into the heart of the East. Its geopolitical origin lies in Palestine. We might be inclined to expect that owing to this position astride East and West, Christianity should have become the religion of West and of East as well. But it has remained the religion of the West.

And the West itself? Has it remained Christian? Can we still speak of a unified Christian West? Undoubtedly not. The non-Christian religions too have gained a foothold in the West —Hindus, Buddhists, expanding Islam. "Go ye and teach all nations." The nations come to us, they teach us, they build temples and mosques next-door to our Christian churches, they have become for Christians a feature of their environment. The religions which used to be restricted each to its own area meet each other within the same space. Why? Because there are no longer any separate spaces, whether for a people, or a culture or a religion. The historical spaces of the several peoples fuse into one universal history. Thus the religions have drawn together; people of other faiths are no longer the "unbelievers" against whom one went to war (not only with spiritual weapons) or foreigners who belong to an altogether different world.

Even in their ideology the religions are no longer wholly separated from each other. Christianity has to a great extent passed on its ideology to the other religions. Nowadays it no longer faces religions which are polytheistic in the *same* sense, or which for doctrinal reasons advocate an absolute caste system in the *same* way, as before they came in contact with it. Thus Hinduism increasingly accepts Christian elements: elimination of the caste system, social responsibility, a trend towards monotheism—without, however, acknowledging these elements as *Christian*. On the contrary: the more Hinduism borrows from Christian-Western thought, the less it is willing to admit a debt to Christianity as such. Likewise Islam is unwilling to admit that Christian influences are at work when modern Moslem society looks upon women in a manner quite different from the ancestral way sanctioned by the doctrine of the Koran. Nor does Islam acknowledge that Christian influences are responsible when it no longer advocates an ideology of "holy war" in the name of the Koran and of the Moslem religion. It claims that this is merely the result of modern Western democratic ideas and of a widespread pacifist ideology. Yet this ideology is Christian. It has developed in the *Christian* West; from Christianity and *from* the West it has spread to the other peoples and to their religions.

And within the Christian West itself? Here too followers of the other faiths rub elbows with the Christian, they belong to his world, they are his friends, relatives and acquaintances. This is the rule, and no longer the exception.

Such is the state of affairs after two thousand years of Christian history. It is a moot point whether this will ever change. But the inquiry into the position of the non-Christian, the person who does not believe, is no idle one. This question is older than the contemporary situation (even though this situation makes it more urgent than ever), it belongs to the faith itself. Why? Because faith tells us: God wills that every man shall be saved, that the message of salvation shall reach every human being, that all may hear it, that no one shall be excluded from the real possibility of this "hearing," no one be allowed to starve for truth, no one be left, through no fault of his own, unreached in the hidden masses of those in "original sin." Faith professes that God's salvific will is *universal*, it gives *all* human beings the real possibility of a relation to God leading to salvation.

Yet it is the same faith which insists that this relation with God is not a matter of personal choice, that it is well-determined and concrete. Faith insists that this well-determined and concrete relation (*religio*) cannot simply be replaced by the individual's good will, that, as a Christian relation, it is the result of a free gift. Faith professes further that all salvation is Christian salvation, that there is no salvation except in and through Christ. So we have a faith which, on the one hand, presents itself as the condition of the possibility of salvation, and, on the other hand, declares that this is offered to everyone, because of the universal salvific will of God.

Let us contrast with this assertion of the faith the situation as we described it above: the great number of those who are not Christians and who do not believe. On the one hand there is the *universal* salvific will of God, which embraces all men; on the other hand there is the indispensable condition of the Christian faith. So we must conclude: if God's salvific will is real, if it presupposes Christian belief and practice, if we may hope that the aim of God's salvific will, man's salvation, will be attained, if not in all men, at least in a majority of them, then we must say that the "others" too are Christians and believers, if by "Christian" and "believer" we understand a person who really reaches salvation through his faith. But may we say this? One who believes that we may not, since in that case he no longer sees any point in being a professed Christian, nor the purpose of missionary activity in the Church, faces an insoluble dilemma. On the one side, there are the countless multitudes of non-Christians and unbelievers who cannot reach salvation; on the other there is the efficacious, universal salvific will of God.

Christians have always faced this dilemma in its main lines, although not with such vivid reality as today. For they have always known of some human beings whom, for merely technical reasons, the Christian message has not reached, and of others who have declined this message, declaring that they were not interested in it, but not in such a way as to justify anyone in attributing their refusal to a culpable attitude which would brand them as rejected by God. How have previous generations solved this problem? By pointing out that God's salvific *will* is not identical with salvation. Should an individual shut his heart to the divine invitation, he would have only himself to blame for his damnation. This would settle the matter, God would have no further obligations. For, according to the *Christian* view prevailing formerly, good will has been lacking in those who do not explicitly profess the Christian religion or have not become Christians in the past. God's universal salvific will is not contradicted if men reject the Christian message.

Thus we may read in the Fathers of the Church that when a man does not believe, it is through his own fault. God's existence is so self-evident, imposes itself so plainly upon man, that although one may overlook this truth for a while, one cannot without guilt do so for any length of time, since the knowledge of God is inborn. In fine, the ancient Church —and, as a rule, the "new" Church too—gets out of the dilemma by saying that in most cases, especially where the Gospel has explicitly *been* preached (hence mainly in Christian countries) the unbeliever is a culpable unbeliever. When speaking of unbelief among Christians, the Fathers of the Church always had only individuals in mind. The existence of such individual instances of guilty unbelief does not give rise to any dilemma or contradict God's universal salvific will. There will always be individuals who are unwilling to listen.

The case is different, however, when the individuals become

a multitude, when a transitory unbelief turns into godlessness, atheism into a permanent state. Can we still say then that such was not God's intention, that it is simply the result of ill will on man's side? To condemn even one individual in the concrete is unchristian. Can we claim that the overwhelming majority of mankind lives in culpable unbelief, is unworthy of salvation, either because by historical accident they are not Christians, or because, living in Christian countries, they call themselves non-Christians and behave as such in our eyes! Dare one who calls himself a Christian consider himself as among the "elect"! What Christian would be so presumptuous? Today we are not presumptuous, we are puzzled, we are inclined to self-criticism, by no means convinced of our own goodness and decency. And are we to count ourselves among the small flock of the elect, singled out from the multitude of those who do not, like us, "deserve" to be loved by God?[1]

How could such a conception be reconciled with the revealed doctrine of God's *universal* salvific will? Does grace grow weaker when it is granted to many? If we are to admit that God offers to *all* men an active grace for salvation, we cannot consider ourselves—only ourselves—as the small flock of the predestined. If, nevertheless, we wish to maintain the necessity of faith, there remains only one possible solution to the problem: man may in faith accept God's universal salvific will and the invitation of his grace, even when to all appearances the opposite is true, and faith seems to be totally

---

[1] The case would remain unchanged if one claimed to have received from God the undeserved grace of Christian faith, so that "deserving" salvation would not come from oneself, but only from God and his grace. For who would have the heart to believe earnestly that God has given this grace precisely to him, and only to him, the explicit Christian?

excluded. And this applies not only to these others, but even to one's own experience, when one thinks oneself an unbeliever, unable to accept the Christian faith. This incapacity might only be apparent, and one misinterprets one's own case.

Let no one say that this is impossible. Today we do not hold it impossible that, notwithstanding a clear contrary impression, a person is in fact not what he thinks he is, because he misjudges himself. He may be convinced of things he seemingly does not accept and led by motives he does not avow to himself. Nowadays all this is rather obvious for everybody. Therefore it is not apriori impossible to say: this man believes that he is an atheist, yet, in fact, he is a theist, and even a Christian theist.

What do we mean, after all, by an atheist? As a rule the answer is: one who denies God, who denies that God may be known in any way whatsoever. There are undoubtedly such atheists, as everyday experience shows. But let us think this over: the atheist denies God. But "God" does not mean this or that reality. When we speak of "God" we mean the ground, the very foundation, of all that is, so that we come into contact with that ground, or stand upon it, or are, so to speak, concerned with it, every time we inquire into anything at all, whatever it may be.

Therefore all questions somehow revolve on this foundation, since it is impossible to consider the things one meets in experience as grounded simply in themselves. For they depend on other things, they stand in a wider network of relations, they do not suffice to themselves. Hence, in this sense, they cannot be their own "ground." Therefore, if there is a ground of everything we meet in experience in a bewildering pluralism, this ground must either be the sum of the realities we meet or

must in some way lie behind these realities. Even should one
leave undecided which of these two conceptions is right, it
would from that point on become impossible to be an atheist.
For this necessary being, which underlies all that surrounds us,
might well be called "God." And since every man, by thinking
and inquiring, always introduces everything in this widest all-
encompassing framework of causal connections—otherwise he
would be unable to inquire, to connect each thing he meets
with the others—he admits something which possesses the
features of what we call "God." Therefore this reality which
is the substrate of everything is the ground of all the realities
we encounter and it underlies every inquiry, every desire to
know, which starts at once from the obvious presupposition
that everything is connected with everything else; hence is
grounded in the same reality. The countless questions of
man are all held together by the conviction that all questions and all answers to a question are linked together, that
they all belong to one system of knowledge, of which every
cognition is a part, in which each one depends on all the
others.

Therefore we are always inquiring into the comprehensive
ground of all reality, whatever may be its precise relation with
the multitude of the realities we encounter; our inquiry presupposes an absolute, all-encompassing, unified meaningful
connection; it presupposes that all our various questions are
borne by one ultimate fundamental question and answer. So
that if the atheist denies "God"—supposing he understands
what is meant by God—he may not or can not any longer ask
any question, since he denies the "ground" of all questions.
He may not and can not ask questions about the weather,
about war or peace, about himself or others, since by denying

God, the ground of every question and of the multiplicity of
that about which questions may be asked, he has also denied
every *possibility* of asking questions; he has denied himself as
the one who asks questions and can not help asking them.
But by denying the inquiry as such, or calling it into question,
he is asking a new question, and he declares that it has a meaning. All this amounts to saying: to the extent to which atheism
understands itself, to that same extent it cancels itself out, it
proves itself logically impossible.

Should the "atheist" reply that this is not the way he conceives God, we shall invite him to tell us how he conceives
him and how one goes about denying something which is nothing in particular, but the ground and the condition of the
possibility of every question and of the rejection of every
answer, without in this very denial entering into relation with
the being he has declared to be nonexistent. We say: to deny
something which is not this or that in particular. Of course,
somebody who has two brothers may deny that he has a
third one, and since this third brother does not indeed exist,
he cannot, by denying him, enter into relation with this nonexistent brother. But in our case we are not speaking of this
or that in particular, a simple datum of immediate sense experience. Therefore, in the present instance, to say: "It does
not exist" can only mean: "What I am thinking of does not
exist." And this may be quite true, especially where "God"
is concerned. But it decides nothing about the question of the
existence of *the* God whom one should "think of," but whom
one generally does not think of. We might even say that
"atheism" generally draws its sustenance from these false conceptions of God. It may be the conception of some kind of
psychic mechanism built into people's heads as the useful and

pedagogically beneficial fiction of the "watchful eye." Then
again it may be that elderly gentleman whom politicians and
Church dignitaries invoke in grave circumstances so as to
surround themselves with an aura of importance, solemnity
and eternity. Or it is the one held responsible when the public
well-being is threatened, to whom petitions and recriminations
are addressed which we call "prayers." He is always the one
who is far away, who remains "invisible," who clergymen
claim will show himself after death, at which time it will become clear that he cannot be mocked. In short, a collection of
primitive infantilisms, of projections of anxiety and the need
for security. What wonder then that there are "atheists"? But
this God, whom *these* atheists deny, really does not exist, and
the fact that many who call themselves theists conceive God
under this guise, in which the atheists wisely reject him, is
yet no proof that the atheists are right. Both groups are wrong:
the atheists who hold that, by denying *this* God as they conceive him, they rightly reject God, and the seemingly pious
theists who speak of a God who, in fact, does not exist.

Is it true, then, that most people today are "atheists," wholly
unchristian, and nothing more? Is the situation really such
—even at first glance—that what is meant by Christianity is
to be found only in a small minority? Or might we perhaps
say that this world which we call unchristian accepts at least
a portion of the Christian faith, a very essential one too, and
has made it a part of its conduct? I mean that portion which
prescribes love for others, the acceptance of others, care for
others. While it is quite true that these excellent virtues are
not practiced always and everywhere, theoretically, at least,
their validity has become universally accepted. And not only
in theory. Who, in past centuries, would have talked about

"integration" or of "help to the underdeveloped countries"? It might, of course, be objected that these ideas are accepted nowadays for merely natural reasons. But even if this were true, where did men get them? Did they manufacture them from whole cloth, all by themselves? Take, for instance, the statement: All men are equal before the law. To most people it sounds wholly secular, profane. Yet is it not derived from this other statement: All men are equal before God? Should we not say, then, that the truth that all men are equal, the precept of universal philanthropy, despite its profane and secular garb, is a seed burst from the capsule of Christianity, which has been carried by the wind into every nook and cranny of the earth, where it is now sprouting and developing into a universally accepted truth? It has struck roots too in the depths of each individual's conscience. How else shall we explain the way people manage to put up with each other? How does it come about that man manages to live with himself, to endure himself, which means that he must accept himself without despair, that he does not despair of this world and its seemingly senseless history, but accepts it, since he keeps working at it? For nobody can accept senselessness as such. That would amount to explaining something by means of nothing.

If one puts up with oneself and others and the world, it can only be because one is aware of something quite different from what one experiences directly, of something which is not senseless. And this experience, which one has at least to some extent —enough at least to enable one to hold out and not to despair —means precisely that which is expressed in a beautiful, unequaled way in Jesus Christ, as the synthesis of the meaningless and the meaningful, because he is the union of the finite and the infinite, of man and God. This experience is the one which is objectively put into words in Christian doctrine. Ultimately it does not matter whether it is interpreted as Christian or not. The experience is there, albeit "anonymously." For by anonymous Christianity we mean that Christianity which is unaware of itself, which does not understand itself *as* Christianity—as we said with regard to Hinduism and other non-Christian religions, which accept Christian elements without knowing them as such. This anonymous Christianity is perhaps not always understood correctly by professed Christians, especially because it stands outside their explicit, official Christianity; often the two may even come into conflict. For it is the fate of Christianity, according to the principles of its history, to be always contradicted, never to be the universally accepted, *explicitly* accepted, religion of man, and nonetheless to keep spreading over the whole world. But if both these things are true, if Christianity is spreading and at the same time not explicitly accepted, we must expect to find Christian elements outside explicit Christianity, whether as the anonymous Christianity of the individual or as the strange phenomenon of a collective anonymous Christianity of whole nations.

We said that it is the fate of Christianity to be contradicted, with the result that professed and anonymous Christianity may combat each other. Why? Do both not mean the same thing? That which is "really" meant shows in the outside forms of Christianity, for every religion needs such forms, needs material manifestations in which it can take shape. These exterior forms may be obligatory and willed by God. Yet it may happen that somebody rejects them, perhaps because they seem antiquated. They necessarily make such an impression, because the concrete features of a religion, on account of their more enduring character, unavoidably lag behind the continual changes in the world, its history and its culture. When one rejects the outside trappings of Christianity, the opposition between anonymous Christianity and explicit, official Christianity grows stronger. Anonymous Christianity becomes ever more alienated from itself, finds it always harder to understand itself.

For the man of today there is an additional difficulty. He who in our planetized world meets the different religions in his own environment, who, as a man of today, has an acute sense of how all knowledge and every religious conviction is marked by relativity, dependent upon factors of perspective and historical circumstance, feels it almost as a scandal that Christianity insists on making absolute claims. And he understands these claims even less easily as it becomes more a matter of his experience that the so-called pagan is by no means less cultivated or less humane than the Christian. And even should he tell himself that absolute claims belong to the essence of religion, that religious relativism would spell the end of all religion, he cannot shake off the impression that these claims are arrogant.

Nor is this the end of Christianity's "arrogance." It makes bold to declare that the concrete, factual essence of man comprises not only his abstract essence as a spiritual person, but also his anonymous Christianity, at least as a possibility of salvation offered from within. Hence Christianity claims that it understands the people who live outside it better than they understand themselves, that their salvation comes from those Christian elements in them which they do not understand and not from that which they themselves consider most important in their life. Of course, another question is how man behaves

towards this, his real essence. How does he experience it explicitly, what does he make of it consciously? Does he know
explicitly what this essence implies, does he know it in such
a way that this *im*plicit, merely "anonymous," Christianity
may also become *ex*plicit Christianity?

There are more questions of this kind. We shall come to
them later. If we turn to the "anonymous Christian" himself,
it is not with the idea that, through some kind of sublime
psychoanalysis, we can "dig up" what is present in the depths
of his being and demonstrate it. This is, of course, impossible.
What we must try to do is this: bring him to realize, bring
home to him, that some of his experiences—some of the things
he knows and feels—are Christian experiences, using also for
this purpose the experiences of others, of mankind at large.

But it is not to the anonymous Christian we turn first. First
we turn to the person who knows himself explicitly as a
Christian. He must grasp the convergence which exists between
explicit and anonymous Christianity. If he grasps it, he can
say, for his own consolation and that of others: That person
there, whether baptized or not, whether a "militant atheist"
or a "matter-of-course atheist," experiences his existence as
that which I experience as Christianity.

2/ The Concept of Subjective Implication

Suppose we have a statement from physics—for instance, the law of gravity. The student of physics cannot know this law without knowing a series of other statements, insofar as these statements are necessarily given together with the law of gravity—as presuppositions or as corollaries.

Not everybody is a physicist or has a talent for physics. Everybody knows what gravity is, but he knows it *without* knowing how this law is established and what follows from it, although this information is "contained" in what he knows explicitly. He knows without knowing that which goes together with what he knows, that which is, from the very nature of things, comprised in it, implied in it. Something which is thus implied only *in some other content* is called an objective implication. An objective implication is a statement which it is possible to deduce from another statement which we know. Yet we know nothing of this implication; although it is contained in the statement we know, it lies beyond the reach of consciousness.

But there is also a subjective implication. Here is my friend, I have known him for years. He is, of course, as

15

a friend ought to be, perfectly reliable. Yet all of a sudden I find out that the opposite is true: the man is unreliable. Then something strange happens. I am not really surprised, I feel that I had always seen the man under *that* light. Not consciously, clearly, explicitly, but vaguely, unreflexively. I always knew that there was something wrong with him. To be sure, I did not know this explicitly, I did not put it into words. Yet it was implied in what I knew explicitly, it was co-known with it. Maybe it would never have emerged into consciousness if some event had not "bumped into" this purely implicit knowledge of mine. Likewise it may happen that we suddenly become explicitly aware of a situation which has been vaguely on the edge of our consciousness. We had never reflected about it before, but a change occurs, the situation deteriorates. And now we put it into words, define how things were before, how our subjective impression has been quite correct: "We knew it all the while!"

So we may say: subjective implication refers to things we have always co-known implicitly, not objectively as expressed in words, so that it often takes some outside influence to make this implicit knowledge conscious and "objective." On the other hand, objective implication is something which is, in a merely negative way, not known, as shown in the example of the person who knows no physics, who is utterly unaware of what is "contained" in a statement of physics. There is no difficulty in understanding objective implication, but subjective implication is not so easy to explain. We understand it only if we conceive of human consciousness as a reality which is not on one plane, not simply two-dimensional; if we realize that it is "constructed" in such a way that it may be aware of things which are not known expressly and thematically, of peripheral contents, of depth contents, of vague or "repressed" contents. Insofar as these different ways of knowing are real, there is subjective implication, as contrasted with what is expressly, thematically known and verbalized.

There are not only different ways of knowing, there are also different ways of living up to what one knows—to what one knows explicitly or only as subjectively implied in what is explicitly known. We are interested only in the subjective implicit, especially in those things which concern the person directly. There are different ways of reacting to some knowledge, we may freely accept or reject it, whether it be explicitly given or present only implicitly. Thus we may refuse for some reason or other to admit that our friend is unreliable, we may refuse to face that fact. It is possible to accept or reject some knowledge not only when it is available in a verbalized, objective, thematic way, but also when it is given only through subjective implication. There are cases where we can and must assume a definite position with regard to the latter kind of knowledge; it is really something which we *know*, which is within the reach of our consciousness, which it must not evade.

Human consciousness contains a variety of elements. Let us consider how many different things make up the content of a human mind, how many different things a man sees, experiences, learns and undergoes. And all this is packed together in one and the same consciousness. If this is true, it follows necessarily that these various contents stand in consciousness in various degrees of clearness. And since they differ in clearness, they vary also in the way in which they challenge consciousness, in which they elicit a reaction from it.

Our point is that not only may various contents be present in one and the same consciousness, but even contents which contradict each other (at least when they are put into words), and that these contradictory contents may nevertheless consciously be maintained even at one and the same time. This is not physical simultaneity in the sense of both contents being verbalized at the same moment. Yet both contents are held onto, even though one may lie "deeper" in consciousness than the other. But since this always occurs in such a way that the explicit statements never face each other immediately, their contradictory nature does not become explicitly obvious.

Here is an example. Somebody accepts as a principle that morality as such does not exist, therefore it does not exist for him. What people call "moral values" are only conventions, outside pressures, not something which obliges absolutely. But the same person sees a child skater on a lake crashing through the ice and about to drown. Does he still think that way in the real "core" of his person, when he risks his life by stepping onto the thin ice to save the child? We said that contradictory contents of consciousness are not thought explicitly at the same time. That is what happens in the case of this man. Before the child who shouts for help all the principles of his ethical scepticism disappear and the absolute obligatory character of decency and morality, which he has always admitted "deep down" in himself, comes to the surface of his consciousness and determines his action. Which will not prevent him, when we point to this action of his, from saying, as he did before: "Absolute morality? absolute obligations? Nothing of the kind exists for me." How is this possible? It is possible because the contradictory contents of consciousness impinge on consciousness at different degrees of vividness. The shouting child has much more impact than the most elaborated theories with their moral scepticism. There is quite a difference, too, in the existential intensity and absoluteness with which such contents are held on to.

But how do we explain that consciousness accepts such a content? How does one come to acknowledge the truth? Is it because the truth "forces" the mind, has but to show itself in words to impose acceptance? Or is it not enough that the truth should shine forth, show itself objectively? Is it also required that the person should *allow* the truth to show itself? Must there not be, corresponding to the evidence of the situation, an openness on the part of the subject, with the result that not every piece of knowledge can force its acceptance on us? That the most momentous kinds of knowledge presuppose for their admission the freedom of their acceptance, the free welcoming of the truth? If this is the fact, if certain acts of knowledge are free acts, moral acts, acts of the will, then the answer to the question how a content presents itself to consciousness depends essentially on how much freedom and what kind of freedom is involved. This involvement of freedom has degrees of intensity and force. We may be indifferent with regard to something, not paying much attention to it; we may be firmly convinced of something; we may also render to something, existentially, the pledge of our whole being, the ultimate commitment of our person.

Language and its distinctions confirm this. For language distinguishes between views and opinions on one hand and convictions on the other hand, between what is merely a wrong opinion and what is really an error. "As I see it," "to my mind" does not mean much. An opinion, whether objectively correct or false, does not grip a person. We may pick it up or drop it without real commitment. When there is such commitment, we speak of conviction, and in the event of a false idea, of error. Nobody picks up a "holy conviction" of a truth in a hurry, and we do not let go of an error without a real struggle. In both cases we have a *basic* conviction. We cannot cling at the same time to a true and false conception with the total commitment implied in such a basic conviction: on that level the choice is between an error or a true *conviction*. But either the true conviction or the error accepted in a fundamental way may co-exist with an "opinion" to the contrary when one of these conscious attitudes reaches only the level of a subjective implication. Man decides for or against God. If he entertains both attitudes, only one of his choices can amount to a basic decision. The other is then of a totally different kind, very peripheral, far from touching the core of the person. Only in this form—as a correct or false view—can it co-exist with the opposite conviction. Only thus can a correct view co-exist with error, a false view with a true conviction.

The question then arises: Is the person always explicitly aware of which, in a determined case, is the "basic decision" —the error or true conviction—and which is merely "opinion" —the correct or false view? In order to know this explicitly one would have to measure the freedom involved in each case, the freedom and the personal commitment which stand behind each decision and have brought it about. Do we have any reflexive yardstick which would make such a comparison possible? Obviously not.

Furthermore, how would one know what is basic decision and what is only shallow opinion, since every statement or conscious content for or against which one decides is only a single item, standing in a consciousness full of such single, and, as we have shown, varied and even contradictory items?

But if human consciousness cannot be considered as an ac-
cumulation of contents simply put together every which way,
one item having no connection with any other; if "consciousness" is always a totality, a collective knowledge possessing a
certain coherence, in which the single items stand in living interaction with each other, complementing, explaining, correct-
ing, interpreting each other, eventually qualifying each other's
contradictory content—how would we then say explicitly and
with certitude: This statement expresses a "conviction," that
one only an "opinion"? All this can be known only implicitly,
for this interaction of the statements is only implicit. We do
not know explicitly how one statement we have in mind is
affected by another which we also have in mind. We do not
know with what implications—subjective and objective—the
statements so color each other that, even though objectively
discordant, they harmonize in our subjective impression, with
the result that both can be accepted, despite the contradiction
they involve. In such a case we do not know explicitly which
of the two statements is decisive.

Not only is there such an interchange between the contents
of our individual consciousness through which they complement each other with implications, there is also such an "interaction" between the collective human consciousness and the
individual consciousness. We might also say that there are
subjective implications emanating from the social milieu. This
is especially true because each individual always wishes, or at
least unconsciously tends, to adapt himself to the environment
in which he lives, the time and the group to which he belongs.
Since he does not want his thinking to be alienated from his
environment he assumes the thoughts of those around him,
explicitly or implicitly. Public opinion, the spiritual atmos-

phere, the style of an epoch—all this is at work, from one person to another, modifying consciousness and what it contains. It is not easy to discover the extent to which this modification is only objectively implicit and how far it may also proceed in a subjectively implicit way. For a person who stands in a merely formal relationship to the authority of another, for instance, blindly accepting what the latter prescribes, the moral quality of the thing enjoined is merely objectively implicit, since he has not the slightest idea of it. If, on the other hand, the relationship to authority is one of well-informed and voluntary docility, although the subject does not yet, on this account, thoroughly understand what is commanded, he has at least some idea of it. For now it is accepted as something which this welcomed and respected authority accepts for itself and personally assumes. And when he realizes that this personal assumption is based on the nature of the bearer of authority and of the action concerned, he must conclude: As I fully trust this authority, so I wholly trust that which it commands.

Tradition is another implication. Take, for example, a statement which refers to a civilized custom, a norm of correct behavior. Even nowadays we still think, at least implicitly: "people" have always acted that way, so we shall do the same. But by doing this we explicitly or implicitly assume as valid certain moral or social ways of behaving, we make them—at least implicitly, by way of subjective implication—the rules of our own conduct. How far this is still explicitly the case today is another question. At any rate, it goes on at least to some extent. Even on the biological level it is impossible for a child to grow up unless he is protected by his parents and his environment and makes use of his elders' experience. He cannot go through their experience all over again, and try everything for himself—how to live in order to stay healthy, what to eat, how to dress.

Likewise man lives from a spiritual tradition, for his life is not long enough to allow him to acquire everything by himself without inherited language, inherited views and ideas. Whatever experience we go through ourselves, to some extent we rely on those who have already gone through it, so that we are their heirs—in an expressly conscious or only in an implicit way, whether by way of objective or of subjective implication.

The same thing is true for metaphysical implications. A person knows about joy, sadness, pain, love. He experiences the feeling of beauty, of repulsion, of release or dejection. But what does he really experience in all this, what is the "core," the "specific" content of these experiences? Does he know explicitly? True, he can reflect on them, but only afterwards. For to reflect means to go back in thought. But going over an experience never enables us to recapture it entirely, to put it wholly and exhaustively back before us. Only the concrete features of the experience are within our grasp, not that which lies beyond them, that which, as metaphysical, cannot become the object of a direct (empirical) experience; that which, nevertheless, we experience in this sense, that it is implied in the explicit (empirical) experience, subjectively implied, hence really known. This knowledge is present even in one who claims not to have it, who calls himself an absolute sceptic. For one who declares that nothing lies beyond the world of bodily experience (that no knowledge of the immaterial is possible), and who advances this claim with the conviction that it is true, has already arrived at that whose existence he denies and whose knowledge he rejects, at metaphysics and truth. For he cannot deny this truth, which is not a datum of immediate sense experience, without affirming it in his very denial.

Or let us take the metaphysical experience of morality. He who declares that nothing of the kind exists, that no one can have such an experience, demonstrates that he has had it. How else could he distinguish between morality and what is not morality? He would be unable to distinguish the two if he had no experience of morality, if he did not move within the horizon of something quite different from the absence of morality, if he could not measure this absence by means of something quite different from it. Hence he has affirmed what he denies *in the very act* of denying it, thus implicitly making a statement concerning it. Of course our sceptic might in the presence of each really moral value declare that he does not simply deny the existence of all morality; he wishes only to point out that the real phenomenon, which actually exists, is misinterpreted by those who defend the objective validity of an absolute order of morality. He might say that what we call morality is in fact identical with individual or collective usefulness, or with what is in some way pleasurable. And he might say that whatever does not bring about such individual or collective usefulness or lead to pleasure, but leads to suffering or pain, is to be distinguished from the useful and the enjoyable; for him the objective basis of morality and non-morality consists in this distinction.

Yet such a sceptic too will behave like the man in the example of the child falling through the ice. In such or similar situations he will—frequently at least—show through his actions, even if not in words and theoretically, that he feels him-

self positively under an obligation, although he sees no usefulness in his action or no possibility of enjoyment. Moreover he
will defend his theory of morality (which reduces the moral
values—for instance, that of truth—to the level of primitive
values) as the only one which makes sense, and he will feel
obliged to stand up for this truth. Thus he will declare that
his ethical system is the only true one. Therefore this moral
sceptic shows that he is getting nowhere with his theory, that,
in spite of it, he believes in an absolute and radical distinction
between what is moral and what is not, and that to a certain
extent he lives up to this distinction.

Because we hold on to a metaphysical affirmation whether
we like it or not, because we become more involved in it, as
we deny it more heartily, we speak of the implication of what
is metaphysically necessary, as of a knowledge which we unavoidably "always already" possess, even when we do not consider it expressly. Thus we always use and know logic too.
He who declares that logic is only a mechanism of our brain, that
there is no logic as such, is already using logic. For the object of logic is thought. He who thinks there is no logic has
already thought logically, he has used logic and used it with
the claim that *this* is the only correct way of thinking. He
does this in the name of the logic which he calls a mechanism,
that might as well have been quite different from what it
actually is. Moreover, although he has to know logic only implicitly—as the tacit, unthematic means for grasping an object
—although he understands nothing about logical principles, he
not only knows formal logic, he even knows ontological logic.
He practices ontology, he treats it as matter-of-course, for
he knows about being. Should he not know being, he would
also be ignorant of the principle of contradiction, which is

based on the notion of "being." But he certainly knows this principle, since he is well aware that when he sits in an automobile he is not sitting in a streetcar. However uneducated he may be, he knows the principle of identity. He understands quite well that, if all men are mortal (if there is an identity between man and mortal), and if he is a man, then he too is necessarily mortal.

Not only is that which is metaphysically necessary always co-known and co-affirmed in every statement, there are also implications of the merely factual, of that which happens to be but does not have to be.

One is an American in fact, not necessarily. One lives in the twentieth century not necessarily but in fact. One might be a German or have lived in the nineteenth century. Hence, whereas metaphysical necessity cannot be thought away, is irremovable, the merely factual might not have been, is merely contingent. The strange thing is that the contingent too is always co-affirmed. We co-affirm our own existence as a fact, not a necessity, we co-affirm the city in which we live, the parents we have, the qualities and abilities we have received. These are all facts; as such they are co-posited, co-affirmed, even though not always with a Yes of full consent. The opposite is often true: because these facts are not necessary (we are not necessarily born of these parents, at this place), they may, in certain cases, utterly irk a person. Precisely these merely factual circumstances bring home to him how questionable, how shaky, how utterly contingent this existence is into which he is called without any necessity, without even the possibility of giving it up. Even should he put a violent end to his life, he would depend for the power to do so on that which he refuses, and thus reassert it *in the very act* of rejecting it. Hence in the same act in which he rejects himself, he asserts himself, posits himself—whether he knows it expressly or not.

Nobody knows explicitly how he relates to himself, although he possesses himself and experiences himself. The same thing holds true with regard to thinking, which everybody experiences since everybody thinks. When a man thinks of the bad weather, he performs an act of thinking. Implicit in this thinking activity is not a theory but some knowledge of the thinking process. If he makes this knowledge explicit, the explicit knowledge will never recapture the implicit knowledge in its wholeness. The same thing applies to the knowledge he has of his being human. He experiences his being human in his corporeity, historicity, sexuality, relation to others, social condition, freedom, personality. He knows *in* this living, better than by any reflexive knowledge, what it means to be human. For however well-elaborated reflexive knowledge may be, it never adequately recaptures what man knows implicitly just by living—by living in a conscious manner; just by enduring himself and others and everyday experience.

Ultimately it is always man himself who lives his life—in love, joy, anger, pain, illness and in death. That is why no theory can express what man ultimately is; he is always "more" than such a theory can put into words. Words cannot express what pain is. Nor can one learn what pain is from subtle metaphysical considerations; one must have pain. Likewise we do not know what anxiety is from the experience others have had of it, but only from our own experience—and such an experience may be far removed from all theories about anxiety. Theories may be important, even necessary, because they may modify the attitude we assume, for instance, towards anxiety;

but real knowledge cannot be obtained from them. It is only because we have this real, implicit knowledge that we have any explicit knowledge at all, so that the latter always lives from the former, as implicit knowledge always, at least to some extent, is transformed into explicit knowledge. But this implicit knowledge does not derive from verbalized, conceptual theories, as if such theories would bring man to what we call "self-relatedness," that attitude towards himself which man must assume in this *or* that manner—that is, freely. For the fact itself of assuming an attitude is not free, it is imposed upon man as the ultimate decision about himself, a decision which is wholly his own, which he can never delegate to anybody else. He may curse this obligation, he may feel "doomed" to it, he cannot shake it off. We might say that man exists precisely in this free choice of his attitude towards himself. For to exist means to know about oneself, in acceptance or rejection. We do not mean a formal abstract knowledge about oneself, but one which is lived in concrete connection with a concrete reality. In such a connection we know about ourselves, and the possibilities of our own nature, we live this nature, we are related to it, we face ourselves in it.

More examples of subjective implication might be considered. The important point is that there is a *subjective* kind of implicit. Since it is subjective it is present to consciousness as co-conscious, co-known, co-affirmed, by way of acceptance or rejection, always as that with which man stands in real contact.

3/ The Transcendental Implication of Being

If we were to expand the title of this chapter we might say: being as that experience in which all our knowledge and willing transcends what falls under our senses; being as that which is always already co-known as the *ground* of whatever can be known. Or we might also say: God as the absolute being about whom we always already know in a subjective implication which is given together with our nature.

For the catechism as it is generally understood, a person knows something about God when he has this knowledge in an explicit, verbalized, thematic way. If he does not possess this express knowledge, it is generally held that the person in question knows absolutely nothing about God. But this is a false conception. In order to understand why it is false, we must get a clear idea of subjective implication as it is explained above. We said that subjective implication refers to things which we *have,* which we always already co-know in unexpressed knowledge, as contrasted with knowledge that is given in an express, objective, thematic way. Therefore we have distinguished two kinds of knowledge. There is a knowledge which man has of things that come to him from without, whether they show themselves directly to him or somebody tells him about them—at any rate, of objects given in a merely aposteriori experience coming from without. On the other hand there is a knowledge which man experiences from within, without any need of an express experience of the kind just mentioned. He simply *has* such knowledge. No need in this case for the reality in question to "present" itself, or for someone to tell him about it. He knows it by himself, he "always already" knows. He always already knows what anxiety is, and fear, joy, love and loneliness; he knows, for instance, the difference between anxiety and fear, even though he might be unable to explain all this. He knows further the difference between his love for his wife and his love for his friend, although he might not be able to put into words wherein precisely the difference consists. This is true although he has experienced both kinds of love, although both occur in him, both are present in his consciousness in their own reality, showing themselves directly to him as part of his subjective self-realization. In a conversation about these things or some other confrontation brought about by the circumstances, he may learn to distinguish these different kinds of love explicitly as well. Yet he has a long implicit experience of what he thus learns explicitly, and all the talking about these matters—the ever more refined concepts and more precisely differentiated expressions—is but a talking after the event about something he has always already known even though he was unable to formulate it.

It is in this sense that we claim that there is an implicit, subjective, unthematic knowledge of God. We realize that it is easier for us to accept, for instance, joy, love, pain as such implicit knowledge than specifically a knowledge about God.

Love, pain and joy are ultimately, by their very definition, states of our own selves, they are already by themselves, in their own reality, in us, in our consciousness, in our personal life. It is perfectly evident, even without depth psychology, that they can be known in the manner of an unreflected, unthematic knowledge. But the situation is different when we say: *deep down* you know "God," you know him necessarily, and even more necessarily than all such events and states of your conscious existence. Against such a claim one might object: but God is not I and I am not God! Therefore it is impossible to experience God in my inner subjectivity as such. "God" is rather by definition the simply unknown, who cannot be directly experienced. Should somebody assert all the same that he knows something about him, then this knowledge must consist of metaphysical considerations and deductions. God might be but the extreme edge, the extreme case, of the purely aposteriori knowledge which we have contrasted with the knowledge called subjectively implicit.

It is obvious that we cannot know "God" exactly in the way in which we know joy, love or pain, in a subjective, unthematic, unreflexive way, or as we experience loneliness or despair, for God is not a determination of our subjectivity. This does not mean, however, that there is no such thing as an inner, necessary, unthematic knowledge of God, not necessarily known reflexively in statements, not of an aposteriori objective kind, a knowledge in the category of a subjective implication.

When we affirm the existence of two kinds of knowledge of God, this should not be understood to mean that one of them might be replaced and made superfluous by the other. Let us rather come back to our example of married love and friendship. One may experience from within that friends are much less exclusively attached to each other than husband and wife, or know in an unreflexive way that friendship may also include a third or a fourth partner, while marriage, of its very nature, does not allow this, and from one's own personal experience with wife and friend, be conscious of these two kinds of affection as thoroughly and basically different; yet even so, in real life all this knowledge, which is only implicit, subjectively implicit, will take shape more quickly if one knows *expressly* and tells oneself that the moral principles which apply to marriage differ from those which apply to friendship. Hence complete true human knowledge supposes reflexive *and* unreflexive knowledge, the original, unthematic experience *and* reflection on this experience. This is especially true in cases where—for reasons we do not have to consider here—the relation between the original, unthematic, subjectively implicit knowledge and its thematic explicitation is rather close. Thus the subjectively known logic mentioned above will hardly ever in any person be present *only* implicitly in such a way that no explicit hint would emerge in this person's objective thematic knowledge.

Moreover, this unthematic knowledge about God which we are trying to establish would not exist if we did not know any objects whatsoever. It is obvious that such subjectively unthematic knowledge of any kind, the knowledge of God included, emerges into consciousness only *with* the objects of aposteriori experience. In *this* sense the apriori, subjectively implicit knowledge of God whose reality we affirm can and must be called knowledge based on sense experience. But the opposite too is true: aposteriori knowledge which comes merely from without assumes a meaning only when and insofar as it brings to consciousness, and refers to, the apriori, subjectively implicit knowledge. Thus, for instance, if we wanted to deduce the absolute validity of the principle of contradiction only from sense experience, to which it is clearly seen to apply, if we wanted to deduce merely aposteriori the truth of this principle, we would not have grasped its real meaning as an *absolutely* valid principle. We must experience it, as it were, "from within," as the apriori condition of the possibility of *every* act of knowledge.

The same is true for the knowledge of God. It becomes a real, solid knowledge about God only when explicit theism—that system of statements we construct about God, the traditional and important "proofs of God's existence"—when this thematic, logically deduced, reflexive knowledge is backed up by that mysterious subjectively implicit knowledge. Nay, in this instance we may say that the express knowledge taken alone is no real knowledge, and that the implicit cognition is the very condition of the possibility of such express knowledge. For as we can make a statement about love only if, behind our statement, stands an experiential knowledge of love—and not the absence of knowledge which we find, for instance, in one who hears of a plant hitherto fully unknown to him—in the same way a reflexive theism is possible only when grounded on and nourished by subjectively implicit knowledge. It is by no means our intention to deny or to belittle the importance of reflexive theism, but we wish to emphasize what it needs as presupposition and background.

But how do we come to affirm a subjectively implicit knowledge about God? If we wish to answer this question, we must start by reminding ourselves that man, as a knowing and freely willing person, possesses some subjectively implicit knowledge about being as such. Everyone already knows in a fundamental way what "being" is,[1] otherwise he would not understand the meaning of this term, and any attempt at a "definition" would remain utterly unintelligible to him. If he can get some idea of what being is when told that a being is that which is not simply nothing, that being is everything which is, which is insofar as it has "being," inasmuch as it is "something"—all this is possible only because in such definitions he is referred to what he knows already, since he knows what "not nothing" is, what "something" is, what is meant by a reality, a thing, a state of affairs, an event or an idea.

One might object against the reality of such ever available, subjectively implicit knowledge that beings and being—that which makes a being a being—are concepts which we do not always already understand, which we have only gathered from experience, through a gradually expanded generalization of the concepts with which we designate what we meet in experience. One might say that, having come to know in experience first a sheep and then a cow, we have subsequently condensed these two notions in the higher concept of a "mammal." The latter has been enlarged into the concept of an "animal," as we subsume fishes, birds, and so on, under this more general concept. This is not the end of our generalizations. We go on to the even more universal notion of "living thing," which includes plants, trees and so on. We take the next step when, under the concept of a "material object," we also put the inanimate things. Finally, we reach the limit of all possible generalization when all that is conceivable—facts, events, states of affairs, feelings, absolutely everything—is put under

[1] I have translated *Sein* by *being* and *Seiender* by *a being* or, when plural, by *beings*. (Translator's note.)

the concept of "something," that is under the concept of "a being." Thus "a being" would be the most general concept, the really last step of such a steadily advancing generalization, the final outcome of all our singular experiences, a concept which covers absolutely everything that is not merely nothing. Because it embraces everything, it is not only the most general, but is also the most empty and the most undetermined, concept. For its content consists in that which is most universal, most empty and undetermined; that is: anything whatsoever, which is called "a being" because it is not nothing, and whose nature is called "being," since "being" is precisely that which makes anything to be.

There can be no doubt that it is possible to generalize in this way—to "abstract," as we say; undoubtedly such an extreme, ultimate degree of abstraction exists. But does this mean that this is for us the *only* way of knowing something about beings and being? Quite a number of philosophers— even within Christian philosophy so called—are of this opinion. They claim that man first knows the individual, concrete things and realities of his inner and outer experience and afterwards performs the generalizing abstraction. Only as its final product does he reach the concept of beings and of being. Against this we declare that such inductive, conceptual knowledge is by no means the only way of knowing about being and beings. We state further that basically, in a subjectively implicit way, everyone knows about being, even if only unthematically. We go even further, we claim that this always already available knowledge of being and beings as such is not only prior to the knowledge of every single thing *as* single (not chronologically but objectively), it is even the necessary, always fulfilled, condition of the possibility of knowing any concrete single object.

Before we examine this assertion more closely, we wish to ask the attentive reader for a certain amount of patience. We ask him to realize that in this subjectively implicit knowledge we have to do with non-objective knowledge, whose content therefore does not stand before consciousness as an *ob*ject. In other words we do not claim that our first knowledge is an *ob*jective knowledge of being and beings, objective in the sense of "thrown before" (ob-jectum) consciousness. In such an express, thematic manner man, in his experience, first faces clearly specific single things—a piece of bread he picks up, a tree he notices, an obstacle in his way. It is with such objects of his experience that he becomes acquainted first, his consciousness is "always already engaged in them." But this is precisely the question: does this "always already being engaged" in certain objects not occur *in* a knowledge (a quite colorless kind of knowledge, which is given, as it were, like some sort of "mood"), in which he knows, in a wholly unreflexive way, about beings and being as such? True, it is not easy to discover this kind of knowledge in oneself, a certain metaphysical power of introspection is required. A person who lacks this power or one who cannot or will not put it to work will never reach this basic proposition of what we consider the only real approach to metaphysics. This much every reader might be expected to achieve: at least to understand the meaning of what we say, even if he is not convinced of its validity. Let him recall the other examples by means of which, in the preceding chapter, we illustrated unreflective, unthematic knowledge of this sort. Once more, our point is: Being and beings are not really "objects" but are "contents" of our consciousness, just as the subjective implication of tradition or of the social milieu, or any other kind of subjective implication, is a content of our consciousness, co-thought and co-known by us, although we are not explicitly aware of it.

It is, of course, not possible to demonstrate our assertion directly. We can only bring attention to bear upon such subjectively implicit knowledge and hope that the reader will allow his attention to be drawn to it. We can only hope that he has, we might say, a knack for metaphysics, so that he is able to grasp that a background knowledge of this kind really exists, a knowledge present to the mind as a kind of "mood," an unthematic "always-already-knowing," although we do not reflect on what is known and cannot push it into the foreground of our consciousness like an object. Let us make an effort to put what we mean more clearly.

First, we have readily granted that we can also gain knowledge of being and beings by the elaboration, after the perception of a specific object, of an express, wholly universal concept of beings and being. We have illustrated such an elaboration, although in a very elementary way, by classifying and comparing the single concrete objects of our experience. Starting from sheep and cow, we have constructed the more general concept of "mammal" which embraces both, and by means of further comparisons and condensations we have gradually risen to the highest concept, the concept of a being. We have repeatedly grasped different realities as different, and while thus grasping the differences we have picked out one feature of the different objects in which they agree, in which they resemble each other. But difference and similarity do not lie *next to* each other, like properties in space, as for instance when two towers have the same circumference and are made of the same material, but one of them is sixty feet higher than the other. These properties, in which the realities we put together under a more general concept are different or alike, stand in a much more complex relationship to each other. Being a mammal is not a property lying spatially *beside* being a sheep or a cow. In the act of distinction there occurs a remarkable separation, not immediately perceptible by the senses, between that which is particular and that which is common.

To put it this way: the act of comparing, of noticing differences and similarities, presupposes that, despite the differences between two objects, we have already considered their different aspects from a common point of view. Hence this act of comparing not only presupposes that objectively something common is *contained in* the things which we compare. It presupposes also in the person who does the comparing some knowledge of these common traits prior to the act of comparing. The common aspects must always already have been grasped "before" (logically, not chronologically!), and in order that, any kind of difference may be noticed. In other words: when I face two things which differ from each other and recognize them as different, the knowledge of the difference presupposes the knowledge of the common features. For I have from the start approached these things with the conviction that they could be compared. Whether the comparison leads me to conclude to a total dissimilarity or to an at least partial similarity does not change anything in the knowledge which, previously to the act of comparing, I have of the comparable and therefore common features of the objects. Even when my act of comparing leads me to notice a total dissimilarity, I have nevertheless put the objects under a common denominator: they are referred to me as I compare them and as I allow them to affect me in their diversity. Hence I state something not only about myself but also about the objects to be compared, I take it for granted that they cannot be absolutely different. For, although I distinguish them as different, such a distinction, to say it once more, is made in the previous knowledge that ultimately they have something in common, that all of them are beings and being. Even when two things *seem* to be altogether and in every respect different from each other, when they *seem* to have nothing in common in any way, however abstract or accessory, even then they have already been put together under one concept, that of "a being."

If there were no such previous knowledge of the ultimate unity of all realities, it would be from the start impossible even to attempt a comparison. It would be impossible to abstract and to construct universal concepts. The highest concept of beings and of being, the general concept which in principle is reached last of all, presupposes therefore some knowledge of beings and of being that is unobjective, absolutely universal and comprehensive. It is only through this knowledge that a comparison is possible which leads to a universal concept. When we say that it is through such knowledge that a comparison is possible, it follows that there is some knowledge that precedes (objectively, not chronologically!) all knowledge about particular things, and is therefore not reached inductively. The fact of the matter is not that I see a sheep, then a cow, and by comparison build up the concept of "mammal" common to both. I did not first know a sheep and later a cow and by comparing the two concepts reach the concept of mammal, which I would then, by a new comparison

with a tree, have extended into the concept of "living thing,"
going on in this way to the final concept of "a being" as the
ultimate thing I can know at all. It is not true that I would
meet the concept of "a being" only at the end of this process.
Hence the course of events has not been what it would have
been if, with the knowledge of the sheep, next of the cow, the
tree, the house, of an idea, a feeling, a fact, there would finally
also have emerged the knowledge of being. Knowledge of an
individual concrete being implies a real knowledge of being
as such. It is true that such implicit knowledge must not and
can not precede these other acts of cognition as explicit objective knowledge. But it is equally true that it does not follow
them by way of some kind of induction. This knowledge is
possessed by the mind, yet not possessed expressly; it is the
more general and basic case of a subjective implication.

We might also put it thus: explicitly man knows beings
only because implicitly he always already knows being. And
not the other way round; it is not as if he knew being merely
as the derived summarization of the single individually known
realities. Being is what is much more originally "there" (although not expressly) than anything expressly "presented" to
knowledge as its thematic and conceptually grasped object.
Being, which is not nothing, and yet, because it is not anything
in particular, seems like an empty space in our knowledge,
does not "present" itself or disclose itself to consciousness. We
"have" it only indirectly, only in and through something else.
Out of this something else it always confronts us in the same
way, always only as that which "makes" this something be,
as that which permeates and fills individual beings in all their
dimensions, so that we cannot assign any place to it among
the multitude of beings, we cannot delimit and outline it, nor

can we separate and distinguish it from anything else. For such a distinction always ranges one thing *beside* another and puts both under a common denominator different from either. But if being itself is this denominator, is distinct *from the start* from everything else and encompasses everything, if it is that in which everything is always already imbedded, then it is impossible for us to make this distinction.

In all we have said thus far, being is considered only from one fixed angle, the angle from which it can be known, compared, distinguished. There are, of course, other aspects of beings and of being as that which is always already unthematically given before any single experience. Thus we always take for granted that every "something," which "is not nothing," may affect our power of choice and of freedom, is something we may either reject or accept. If it is true that we cannot speak, think, or act without having to do with "being," since there is no occurrence which is not an occurrence in being; if it is true that no inquiry is possible—about food or drink, about our work, our joy or our anger, about this or that person or ourselves—which does not necessarily, if unthematically, include the question of being *as* an element of every inquiry about anything whatsoever; then it is only in the context and the light of being that we can inquire about and think of all things and everything, that we can act in any circumstances.

We must, then, react to every being whatsoever as to a being *as* such, whose concrete individuality is always already *in* our very reaction taken in a system of co-ordinates, an absolute context, the context of our unexpressed knowledge of being as such and as a whole. If in fact our every reaction to an object orders this object at once in this "system"—if, for instance, we always already take for granted that it is impossible for something to be and not to be at the same time, or to be itself and its opposite at the same time; if we take for granted that fundamentally we have the power to inquire about everything, and thus to know everything (otherwise the inquiry would be impossible for us); that everything, if considered from the correct angle and within the total system of reality, can be the goal of some striving and is therefore good; if we take all this and much more always already for granted, we are led to the following conclusion: we can react to the single objects of our experience only in the light of this always already available, though unexpressed, pre-knowledge of being as such and as a whole.

On the other hand, it follows also that such a subjectively implicit knowledge of being can never emerge in a way which is chronologically or objectively independent of our experience of concrete individual objects. We do not first know about being in general, purely in itself, and then use this knowledge in order to recognize individual things (in the way in which we use our knowledge about camomile to make tea with it). Rather we become aware of this unthematic, vague, non-conceptual knowledge of being only *in the act of* thematically proposing to our consciousness a specific object which affects it as a determined individual object and is recognized as such. In other words, the comparing, unifying, distinguishing, and hence knowing, subject always already carries within him the knowledge of "being" as the apriori criterion, as the perspective, the system, the horizon against which he knows the empirically given individual object in its singularity.

Although it is apriori with respect to the single object, this criterion is not an arbitrary subjectivity of the knower. It is subjective insofar as it grounds the spiritual nature of the knowing subject, insofar as it is given together with it, determining its inner structure, constituting the "horizon" against which the spiritual subject at once sees things and "thus" knows them. But since it is precisely on account of this apriori ontological structure that the subject is the being which grasps single things objectively—that is, which distinguishes them from each other in their difference—this subjectivity is radically objective, objectivating, and universally valid.

Since we are not writing a theory or a critique of knowledge we need not investigate this criterion more thoroughly. It will be enough to characterize it as the inner apriori structure of the spiritual existent, the spiritual subject; as the apriori law of that which a being of its kind may know, of that with which it is related, as the object of its knowledge—what scholastic philosophy calls its "formal object"; that is, the object towards which a certain cognitive or striving power tends of its very nature, to which it is, as it were, "attuned." Thus we can say of the ear that it is attuned to sound, so that sound is its formal object, as color is the formal object of the eye. This is because the structure of the ear and that of the eye have from the start established sound as the possible object of knowledge for the ear and color as the possible object of knowledge for the eye; because eye and ear are built in such a way that they take in certain things and not others. We might say that the very structure of every power of knowledge involves a factor of discernment, a selective principle with which it perceives, judges, takes in its material object from among the multiple things which impinge upon it. This selective principle works like a filter. The object which gets through it is admitted, while the remainder is rejected at once. Thus there are, as our example of eye and ear has shown, cognitive or striving powers which possess only a finite, limited formal object, a selective principle which is not open for everything.

Of course, the question of the formal object of the spirit, of human knowledge, is very much under discussion, especially between Christian scholastic philosophy and German idealism on the one hand and the so-called critical philosophy of Kant on the other. Kant claims that the *formal* object of the understanding, of the human spirit, is finite and limited, that the apriori criterion with which human knowledge meets objects is a criterion applying only to the objects of physics, to spatio-temporal reality; hence man can discover nothing about other realities through his critical understanding. On the other hand, classic philosophy, the so-called *philosophia perennis,* which, in this respect, comprises Greek and Christian philosophy and German idealism, claims that the formal object of the spirit is really, and not only presumptively, unlimited; that is, that man's horizon, within which he takes in the objects given to him aposteriori, is absolutely infinite.

We shall briefly discuss this problem, although in a very modest way and not as thoroughly as its importance warrants. Since it involves practically the whole of the critique and of the metaphysics of knowledge, we can within the scope of our considerations mention only what we deem most important. Let us stay with the example which we have already considered and ask ourselves: does the ear know that its selective principle (sound) is limited and limiting, so that it observes, for instance, that color lies outside its grasp? Obviously not. For if the ear could note that it hears only sounds and no colors, it would have at least a negative idea of something which is not a sound. Hence we must say that a knowing power whose formal object is really finite cannot discover the finiteness of this formal object. A finite system as finite cannot make the finiteness of this system, hence this system in its totality, into its own object. In order to grasp a system's finite nature as such, the knower must stand in a higher system, for he can know the finiteness of a certain finite system only by means of, and from the vantage point of, a more comprehensive system. Therefore a finite formal object means that the knowing power specified by this formal object cannot recognize its own finiteness as such. It is precisely because the ear, by its very structure, perceives only sounds that it is apriori unable to conceive of anything which is not a sound. For only by being able to know something else would it know the finiteness of its own formal object.

What, then, about man and his knowledge, which uses universal concepts? Suppose that his knowledge is restricted to that which is in space and time? We would then have to find out how he is aware of this! Although in many respects he is bound to space and time, the very fact that he is aware of his condition implies that he has at least a negative notion of something which is above space and time. When man inquires and wonders about himself, when he realizes that he is restricted to a certain domain of being, he thereby shows that his knowledge cannot be restricted to a limited domain of being. By contrast, the mistakes of a finite computer, being the mistakes of the whole computer as such, cannot be "recognized" and corrected by it. When man states that there are realities, or at least that he can think of realities, which are apriori beyond his reach and that of his knowledge, he has already become one who is concerned with these realities, he has asserted something quite essential about them, he knows them at least from a certain point of view, namely as realities unknowable for him. Hence we may say that in knowing a limit as limit man has—at least in a certain sense—already transcended this limit, he already operates with a "system," a criterion, a horizon which lies beyond mere spatio-temporal singularity. And even should we admit that this self-transcending, this questioning, this awareness of our own finiteness occurs in virtue of a system which, although higher, remains finite, hence not self-explaining, the very fact that we know it as finite, and we inquire about it, shows that we are already beyond it. We have transcended the allegedly finite spatio-temporal horizon and expanded it into an unlimited horizon whose object is not the limited, merely local formal object, but all conceivable and possible realities—in short, all that exists, being as such.

"Being" as the unlimited horizon, as the unrestricted formal object of his knowledge, is not known thematically by man except when he makes it expressly into the theme of his consideration, as we are doing right now; it is given only as non-objective, subjectively implicit knowledge. This knowledge, as we have said, is in some way colorless, diffuse, comparable to some kind of "mood." The situation is like that in everyday life, where we are also not always expressly aware of our mood, where it is often only afterwards that we notice that our basic mood was cheerful, or depressed or disgruntled, although all the while we were meeting objects out of this awareness and within this mood. Of course, the "attunement to being" should not be understood in the sense of an arbitrary, subjective disposition, like the one by which man experiences the state of his body without reflecting upon it. We mean rather a spiritual, or as it is called, an "intentional" attunement,[2] a kind of inner clearness, a "luminescence" out of which and by means of which we concern ourselves with a single determinate object. We mean the atmosphere, the "space," within which we allow objects to meet us. This attunement to being, this facing of being, is also called a "basic disposition" (*Grundbefindlichkeit*). We always already know about being and beings; we always already tackle individual objects with this unreflexive, unuttered, presupposed knowledge, we arrange them in this system of co-ordinates which is never thematically known, we "treat" them as beings, as things that are interconnected, interdependent, distinguishable from each other, as realities which we can accept or reject, which have something to do with our knowledge, our will and our freedom; as something which by itself can never wholly fill the infinite expanse of our knowledge, since the formal object of this knowledge is being and beings as such. Hence when single objects are known as single, as determined, as well-defined— that is, as limited—they are always already arranged within the previously known, unlimited, all-encompassing totality which alone makes possible the experience of individual things as individual, since we experience the individual, determined, limited object only by transcending it in the direction of the

[2] The translation of *Gestimmtheit* as *attunement* is borrowed from the excellent German-English glossary appended to the book of William J. Richardson, *Heidegger: through Phenomenology to Thought* (The Hague, Martinus Nijhoff, 1963, p. 700) which we have frequently used for this translation.

unlimited. We call this transcending, this knowledge which always already reaches beyond the single object, the "transcending anticipation" (*Vorgriff*).[3]

If we wish to describe the nature of this transcending anticipation, we might say that it is the transcendence towards the totality of all the knowable inasmuch as it is presupposed by every single act of knowledge as a condition of its possibility. We might ask once more: why does this transcending movement go out towards the totality? (We have already touched on this problem from another angle.) Why cannot one or several single realities be that towards which knowledge strives prior to any single act of knowledge? As we have shown above, should the transcendence aim at a single object (or even at several such objects) simply standing near each other, it would not make possible a comparing or distinguishing of them. If the transcending anticipation aimed at many particular objects, we should inquire whether it aims at them as *disparate* objects, without any connection. This hypothesis is excluded at once, since the very fact of calling the objects absolutely disparate puts them at once together, not only because all of them are known as disparate, but also as having objectively nothing whatever to do with each other. This supposes a common ground in all of them, since nothing cannot be the ground of something; it supposes that they have something in common, that they are not simply disparate. If the anticipation cannot aim at several things as *disparate*, we must find out whether it unifies this plurality. In that event

---

[3] This corresponds to the *excessus* of St. Thomas Aquinas, to the *dynamism* of Maréchal and to *the pure desire to know* of Lonergan. (Translator's note.) For a further study of it, see E. Coreth, S.J., *Metaphysik*.

the apriori principle of the unity of this plurality would be
that which in reality is the formal object of the anticipation.
Then we are back at our thesis: unlimited being is the "whereunto" of the anticipation. Every single object as such would
by definition be the object of our inquiry *together with* other
objects, so that in every inquiry about an object there would
be affirmed the legitimacy of another inquiry, the inquiry
about the pluralism of inquiry. But such an anticipation, insofar as it is *known,* presupposes a unity of all inquiries. It implies that underlying every explicit question there is a unique
question which is always already answered, yet always remains open—the question about being as a whole. That is why
we might also say that the object and the origin of every question as such is like the "whereunto" of the anticipation: the
question does not aim at any single object and does not
originate from it, it transcends it towards "more," towards the
whole of the "inquirable" as such, even as the anticipation
transcends every individual reality in the direction of the
knowable as such.

What shall we say, however, if the claim is made that the
anticipation aims at the void, that nothingness stands at the
beginning and the end of each question, that one who goes
on asking questions, and trying to know always more, finally
ends in the void of nothingness? We would reply with a question: how can mere nothingness be the moving force and the
goal of a reality, of the anticipation or of the question? Since
by definition nothing means "not anything," how can what is
absolutely nothing open up, as it were, the horizon of the
"inquirable" and of the knowable? But if we conceive the
object and the scope (both mean the same thing) as the absolute space of the question, we *have* already conceived them

as a positive reality, as something which *is,* which cannot be nothing.

But what if someone should claim that the object and the scope are but the objectivated projection, as it were, of the fact that our mind stops nowhere and never, the objectivation of the fact that we are unable to stop our questioning at any object? As a first approximation, we might put it that way. Once more we would say that, in this thrusting "ever further," in this "never arriving," never being satisfied, in this steady asking and inquiring, in this endless restlessness, in this dynamic infinity the spirit experiences its own nature. But the question remains: what is the sense of this unlimited openness if there is nothing onto which it can open? It would be a dynamism into emptiness and nothingness. But pure nothingness cannot put something in motion, it cannot raise a question.

What have all these considerations to do with our assertion that man has a subjectively implicit knowledge of God, one which does not replace the thematic, explicit knowledge of God, but without which this explicit knowledge could not exist?

Let us first summarize what we have said. Man as a spirit always already faces being as a whole. From the beginning man encompasses in this apriori "attunement to being" the unlimited fullness of possible objects. In other words, every time he tends towards a single object, he aims in an endless movement of his spirit at the totality of all possible objects. Hence in this fundamental movement the spirit affirms that this unlimited fullness of all single objects can be put under a universal, unlimited all-encompassing concept of being, since this fullness of particular realities is undergirded by the original unity of being, which supports and unifies the multiple unity and the unified multiplicity of particular objects, as its ground and origin. The transcendental movement of the spirit which is given in this attunement to being aims ultimately at the original, unlimited, absolute unity of being as such—as opposed to the single limited existents. This infinite reality which is absolutely one despite its infinity, this ground and origin of the whole diversity of finite particular beings, is called "God." Hence God is the goal of the transcending movement of the mind which has always already passed beyond any particular object and only thus recognizes individual objects as individual. In this way God is always already co-known in the subjectively known infinity of the horizon of the human spirit. He is known not thematically, not explicitly in propositions or conceptual knowledge, not as an inner peculiarity of our subjectivity, as we implicitly know a pain. On the other hand he is not simply given like a single object, hitherto unknown, suddenly revealed and made known to us aposteriori. In this unlimited transcendental motion towards being as such, God is present as the all-encompassing and undergirding ground of this unlimited fullness of possible individual beings. We may also say: in the transcending anticipation, in this openness of the spirit towards being and beings, in this unlimited luminosity of the spirit, in this attunement to being which, unlike every single content of consciousness, is essential to man, God is present in a subjectively implicit and unthematic way. He is the asymptotic limit of our striving; that is, the being towards which this movement of the spirit, the movement through which it grasps all its objects, strives as towards the goal that attracts it, a goal never reached because it is situated at an infinite distance.

This should make it easier to understand what we mean by
claiming that there are two kinds of knowledge of God, or,
if this helps to avoid misunderstandings, two moments in the
one and total knowledge of God: on the one hand the reflexive,
aposteriori knowledge which we look for when we present the
so-called proofs of God's existence; on the other hand, the
knowledge of God rooted in the permanent subjective attunement of man, in his transcendental formal object, being pure
and simple. And it should be evident, too, that the latter
knowledge of God, the unthematic subjectively implicit knowledge, is the indispensable prerequisite, the necessary condition
of these proofs of God's existence, insofar as in such proofs we
reach a notion of God only when we grasp the idea of an
infinite being. For should we not grasp such an idea, we would
only reach an antecedent finite cause of a finite observed
reality, something which is definitely not "God." Hence if we
wish in such a demonstration to reach God as God, it is not
enough to admit a first cause, we must also acknowledge this
first cause as the infinite being. But this acknowledgment derives from the fact that man has from the start and necessarily
that knowledge which grasps the single object as single object,
that is as a finite object, in an apriori transcending anticipation
towards the infinite as such. Otherwise he would not know the
finite as finite, nor would he be able to know that such an infinite being can be conceived as possible.[4]

[4] One might object—as has been done, even by Christian philosophers such as Geyser—that we may discover the finiteness of a finite
object by comparing it with another finite object. Thus we may see that
one tree is not as tall as another, and hence know that it is finite, since
compared with the other it is smaller, hence more finite. But then the
question arises how we can arrive at this conclusion. In order to know
two finite realities in their mutually related finiteness, it must first be

But if the affirmation of God and the vindication of such an affirmation is based on the undeniable knowledge of an infinite being, the thing we call "transcending anticipation" towards the infinite can no longer be ignored as an interesting but highly problematic speculation. In this event such a transcendence, or what it implies, is undoubtedly that which must stand *behind* any express knowledge of God whatsoever, if that knowledge is to be a real knowledge of God. Then we must say that man knows God explicitly and really only because implicitly he always already knows being. On the other hand, it does not follow from the fact that man possesses this implicit knowledge about being that he always, already, and to the same extent, possesses an explicit knowledge of God. But we may reject as false the widespread opinion that the man for

---

possible for me to compare them. This supposes that I grasp and know both objects under one common aspect before any comparison of their concrete properties and finiteness. Of course two finite realities, when juxtaposed and compared with each other, possess common properties, but we cannot perceive these common properties as such immediately with our senses. The common features and the differences are not separated, they do not lie simply beside each other like two colored spots. We can discriminate in this way that which is common from that which differs only by using a common, apriori angle of comparison, which derives from our own spiritual nature. We use this angle naturally, subjectively; not, however, in a subjectivistic way, which would mean in a purely arbitrary way, lacking all objective validity. From this point of view we compare the two realities, we use it as the absolute criterion to discover the finiteness of two finite objects as distinct from each other. Hence if comparison presupposes a knowledge of comparability, and if this knowledge is possible only when we already know beforehand whereunto we compare, under what aspect, criterion, horizon, then this apriori, universal, universally valid horizon of being which is always already known by the subject is not only the condition of the possibility of knowing the infinite—that is, God—it is also the condition of the knowledge of the concrete finite being.

whose explicit thematic consciousness God is not a datum knows nothing whatsoever about God. For God as the *ground* of all that which we know is always already co-known, through what we call the transcendental implication of being or of the mystery of being. It is true that being, since it illuminates everything, is utterly obvious, presents itself as that which, by gratuitously giving itself, makes us exist and know things; yet it gives itself as that which is, in a sense, not-given, as that of which we cannot dispose, as that which is not measured, since it is itself the measure of everything (how could it then measure itself?), as the uncomprehended which comprehends everything —in short, as "the mystery." So when we speak of the implications of being as the mystery, we mean: the implication of that which orders everything and cannot itself be ordered, of that which measures everything and is itself not measured, of the all-encompassing which is not encompassed, of that which does not speak, yet whose voice cannot be ignored, which lies hidden and cannot be overlooked; the implication of that which is always and everywhere present and available, which "surrounds" man not as air surrounds a rock but in the way in which spirit as such surrounds—that is, by being the vehicle and ground of all man's knowledge. For the mystery of the absolute spirit moves the spirit in all its activities both as its innermost core and as that which stands infinitely far above it. Even when man concerns himself with the most trivial details of life, he can do it only because he transcends it in a movement towards the fullness of the ungraspable, towards the mystery of God.

4/ The Experience of God as The Mystery

In general we term "mysterious" something which it is difficult for us to grasp, a problem which reality offers to us
without at once yielding its solution. When the problem is a
religious problem, we call it a "mystery." Catholic theology
distinguishes mysteries in the wide and in the strict sense.
Mysteries in the wide sense are statements which are mysterious, whose content—the compatibility of their terms—can be
grasped only with difficulty or not at all, but whose truth—the
fact that such is really the case—can be discovered by natural
reason. This is possible because these statements refer either
to the existence of God as it can be known by reason or to
finite realities, not to God as God. Mysteries in the strict sense
are statements whose truth can be known only by a special
revelation of God and whose inner possibility cannot be
grasped by the human mind even after such a revelation. Dogmatic theology knows of three absolute mysteries, *mysteria
stricte dicta:* the Trinity, the Incarnation and supernatural
grace. The other mysterious statements of Christian revelation
may be considered as deriving from these three basic mysteries.
Thus transubstantiation, the substantial transformation of the

bread into the body of Christ, insofar as it is an absolute mystery for every finite spirit, is a consequence of the Incarnation.

We understand a "mystery" in the theological sense only if we understand it as an *enduring* mystery, not—as is usual with us—as a problem we might solve, a difficulty we might untangle, if only our reason and insight were not so restricted and relative. In that sense a "mystery" would be something provisional, something we have as yet to grasp. That which by its very nature is a "mystery" always remains a mystery. It would not be a mystery if we were ever going to be able to understand it.

We are used to identifying "knowledge," "intellect," "rationality" simply with that lower kind of knowledge which consists in discovering the necessary connection between propositions, whose content itself is given to us in clearly defined and determined concepts, notably in logic, mathematics and the exact sciences. But such "rationality" is a spiritual operation of a secondary kind. We have already explained that all knowledge is borne by the "dynamism" of the intellect to being as such, by that anticipation which no longer comprehends or fathoms this unlimited fullness of reality in absolute unity, but which is gripped and overwhelmed by being. At the very root of every act of knowledge, as its foundation, there is a reference to the undefinable, the unutterable, the "mystery." Spirit is that which is consciously in the grip of the ungraspable as such. We may refuse to accept this, ignore it and use this transcending anticipation only as a tool for the everyday knowledge of that which lies within the mind's grasp or horizon. We may also advert to and freely accept this dynamism which points towards the incomprehensible. But the human spirit always lives from this unuttered infinite onto which it opens, by which it is grasped, but which it cannot itself grasp or appropriate. At all times man, not only as an intellect but also as a whole human being, is drawn by the Incomprehensible—in his freedom, in his "heart," in the most intimate and radical center of his personal existence.

If "mystery" does not mean only the provisional—what is not yet known, the not yet elaborated part of our knowledge —if it is instead something which endures, then it does not only affect man's relation to God during this present life. God as a mystery is also present when man stands *im*mediately before God, when he has an intuition of God "face to face."

Otherwise it would not be true that God, of his very nature, is *the* mystery. He is the mystery as such, because he is the infinite fullness of being, because he is the goal towards which the finite spirit always transcends itself in its dynamism, without ever comprehending or grasping or fathoming this end of its transcendence. That is why the Christian doctrine of faith says expressly that even in the beatific vision God remains the ungraspable in his "incomprehensibility." This means that man has reached the peak of his knowledge when he possesses the unfathomable in absolute proximity and immediacy and knows him as unfathomable. As long as this supreme perfection of knowledge is not reached in the present life, man may err about the true depths on which his knowledge is grounded, he may overlook the fact that he always already stands open towards the mystery, that it is not the limitation of single objects, but the unlimited fullness of the mystery, which basically determines his nature. Should the unlimited not be the ultimate ground of what man is, he would be unable to experience his limitation as limitation. As long as man has not yet fully achieved and welcomed his nature, he can fashion for himself an "image" of the mystery cut down to his own size, he can ignore that which he experiences as the most incomprehensible, and at the same time as the most central, element of his thinking. He can do all this. But he cannot shake off the grip of the mystery. Therefore the question is not: *Does he* experience the mystery, does he unescapably experience it as the basis of all clear and certain knowledge? The question is: *How* does he experience it?

The man of our time, prompted by an existential need arising from the religious problem, likes to relegate his experiences in this respect to a domain where he believes them to be no longer threatened by the "intellect." He is convinced that what he has experienced belongs to a wholly "irrational" realm of experience. He feels this way because he identifies intellect and reason with the well-defined and intuitive knowledge of the separate sciences, without noting that such "clear" knowledge is carried by the dynamism of his intellect towards the ungraspable mystery of being as such. In reality the mystery affects the whole person, so that experiences deriving from its attraction actualize everything in man. Hence we cannot ascribe them, say, to joy alone or to anxiety alone or, as the rationalist says, simply to a particular contingent manner of thinking which provides us with a "philosophico-metaphysical" interpretation of existence.

On the other hand, we should not try to verbalize the experiences of which we are speaking or confuse them with their conceptual formulation. These are "transcendental experiences," that is, they are always given as the prerequisite condition for the knowledge of each single object. We have them when we look away from them towards the single object, it is impossible adequately to bring out the "totality" which is present in them, or to put it *beside* some other object and contrast it with this object. One who grasps the notion of subjective implication undoubtedly understands that there are data of consciousness which are not primarily and originally known through a thematic reflection on them.

In order to see this more clearly, let us have a look at what we may call the "experiences of transcendence." We know of experiences of anxiety, joy, sadness, yearning, hope which refer not to a specific "something"—illness, money, or anything of this kind—but, as it were, to "everything and nothing," which are undergone, so to speak, in their pure openness as limited by nothing. Such experiences are not reflexively undergone. Expressed, verbalized anxiety, for example, is no longer the headlong, drowning plunge into the bottomless depths of existence, it is a cheap twaddle assuming a tragic air. But *in* the real, original experience man stands open for the reality itself, although, or rather *because* it is inexpressible, it is the mystery. Only afterwards does this real experience emerge in some kind of makeshift explicit reflection upon itself, although it constitutes the very basis of such a reflection. We should not underrate this experience as "irrational," for it is the root of all knowledge. Suppose that somebody claims that it makes no sense to try to find out whether a thing is false or true. What takes place in such a case, even though unthematically and by way of subjective implication? Not only is the person in question already reflecting, he assumes implicitly as the basis of his reflection the existence of truth, of a distinction between truth and falsehood, and of meaningfulness. For only in the supposition that there is such a thing as meaningfulness can he hold that nothing makes sense, that this statement contains more truth and meaning than its opposite. One who reflects on the experience of transcendence does not then for the first time come into touch with it, for the experience has always already taken place. Were this not the case, were this experience not the foundation, the prerequisite, we should be unable to reflect upon it. It is impossible to reflect on "time" without referring to the original experience of "time." It is only by referring constantly to the experience we have already had, towards which reflection can only point, that we "understand" what "time" is.[1]

We have said of the experience of mystery that it is one which affects the whole human person, hence one which, it would seem, it would be difficult to overlook. Yet it is often overlooked. Precisely because it is given as the foundation of even the most trivial experience, we tend to ignore it. Never does it clearly contrast as such with other experiences, except when it is present in great intensity. It is only given like the light which makes other things visible without itself being seen. That is why it requires a total openness on man's part, a full commitment of the will, a real training, to observe this experience, to let it emerge, to acquiesce freely in this basic disposition of our spiritual existence and not run away from it towards more "solid" realities whose bodiliness is always around us. But it is only when we give free rein to this basic experience of the mystery and do not repress it, when we stand poised, without vertigo, before its coming, that we reach the real and unique truth of existence, instead of losing ourselves in the empty multiplicity of separate truths.

[1] Do we really understand what "time" is? It is enough to try to explain it to somebody else in order to convince ourselves how little we understand what "time" really is.

It is simply not a fact that what is really true must "dawn upon" everyone. Truth has not yet been experienced by one who has had only those experiences undergone and explicitly acknowledged by everyone. On the other hand, something is not necessarily untrue because it is the recognized and acknowledged experience of only a few people. This makes it clear that, properly speaking, every philosophical problem is a moral problem, because it involves seriousness and patience. Further, that everybody experiences as his truth only that which fits in with his endeavors, his existential commitment. If we go on to inquire *how* man experiences the mystery, we would be inclined to answer: as it suits him. Take a wise and a stupid person. For the wise person reality is filled with mystery. To be sure, the stupid person too experiences mystery as that which passes his comprehension. But for him what he does not know and never thinks about is something remote, from which he turns away, because it is held not to concern him. This is "stupid ignorance," which—with its indifference to the incomprehensible and its proud infatuation with what can be observed and controlled—is always of the opinion that somebody somehow must "see through" all these things. The wise person, on the other hand, knows that he knows nothing. For what he knows is riddled with ignorance. And this ignorance follows him always and everywhere, surrounds him from every side, enters with its nocturnal darkness through all the flaws of existence. This is not stupid, but learned ignorance (*ignorantia docta*). For it, the unknown is not simply what one has no information about, what lies on the other side of the wall. It does not say: "What I do not know does not concern me." It does concern me, I do experience it. The mystery is, for man, and thus for everyone who considers himself human

—for the wise person—not what is absent, not what lies outside consciousness, but what is given, but given *as* mystery; that which is nearby, that which sustains and shelters; nay, that which is loved. It is not the thing which limits and restricts his knowledge, but that which raises it to real infinity, releases and "frees" it, because, as we shall see presently, mystery as such gives itself in absolute proximity as grace.

Man speaks of the experience of the mystery, and he can do so only in concepts which are, by their very nature, only byproducts of the original experience. At best he may make a negative statement and say: The absolute being is not one single being beside others within a common horizon, the unlimited is not limited, the incomprehensible cannot be comprehended, the uncontrollable cannot be controlled, and so on. But in this way reality is expressed indirectly, through subsequent reflection. The original experience itself, on the other hand, is not the subsequent determination of an object by means of concepts which are added to it from without. It presents us with a "negativity" which is in fact highly positive, namely, the transcending of every single object, the dynamism which passes beyond every finite reality and its concept.

But now we must mention a determination of the mystery which, although of human origin, hence merely "analogous," is nevertheless most important with regard to the conduct befitting man in the presence of the mystery towards which he ceaselessly transcends himself. The mystery as such, which we call God, is a "person." Therefore when man has an experience of God, it is an experience of God as personal—as HE, not as an impersonal IT. "God" is in fact conceivable only as a person. For person means: self-consciousness, self-positing, freedom, decision. Since such features belong to a person and are found in man (insofar as he is a "spirit" and differs from infra-spiritual creatures by possessing these features) we do not see why we should not ascribe them to "God." Because it is in his being as a person, in his knowing and free self-presence, that man experiences the mystery as the imponderable ground of his most essential activities and of the realities he encounters, he cannot deny the personal character of the mystery unless he is ready to bring it down to the impersonal status of infra-human reality, thus denying that it is the ground of the human person. When man acknowledges that the God-Mystery is a person he does it, of course, in a way which surpasses every individual human experience, so that every name of God, even the most positive (such as "Being," "Ground"), is lost in the abyss of the Mystery. Only in this sense, but in this sense really, should God be called a "person": the absolute fullness and brightness of self-presence and of freedom, as against every single being in its limitations.

If the divine Mystery is a "person"—a person in such an absolute way that we can no longer form an idea of it—man stands before the person of God within the sphere of the mystery. We may also say that he is confronted with the freedom of God, for he does not stand before a static being whose properties, especially with regard to his conduct towards man, are governed by some factual necessity. He stands before a being of absolute power, infinity and mysteriousness, who goes to the encounter with man as freedom, and in this sense as a "person." When we say as freedom, we mean that since God is a free person man cannot by his own powers work out *how* God must behave towards him. We can order things as we will and to some extent dominate them. A thing has specific properties, and when we know them, we know where we stand in relation to that thing. Not so with a person, who is the absolute and lasting mystery, not so with the Mystery who is a person.

True, the attributes of this person are also specific inasmuch as, being the necessary properties of God, they cannot be differently conceived or thought of as not existing. In this sense, for instance, the attribute of infinity or of absolute self-presence is not within the sphere even of God's freedom as a person. But the ways in which these attributes come to bear upon us are free and, therefore, not previsible for us from without. That is why man cannot foresee what is in store for him in the events of life. He may perhaps consider certain possibilities, as we do with regard to somebody we do not yet know intimately, about whom we may nevertheless say in general that (since he is a person, and so a free agent) he might agree to make himself known, or again he might decide to forego all communication. He may follow either course in love or in hatred, in friendship or in hostility. Hence we may construct a certain system of possible or conceivable modes of behavior, although when God is in question it is impossible, owing to his incomprehensibility, to say merely apriori, from an examination of concepts, whether the particular way of acting we have thus outlined is actually real or concretely possible.

Yet when we examine such a system, we might say: either God is near us or he is far from us, although this nearness or remoteness may not at once be interpreted as love or hatred, friendship or hostility. When we consider that creation means production by the fullness of reality and of being, we may conclude that when God puts a creature into existence he owes it to his own holiness to treat the thing he has made with a certain benevolence, and even to love it. This love does not imply God's calling his creature to the kind of nearness which is a matter of conscious experience. There is also a love that, measured with a more absolute criterion, is experienced as the overawing benevolence of the supreme creator, a love in which a secluding remoteness is preserved. It may retain this character because it is expressed in silence, or because it is misinterpreted or because man does not know what to do with it. Moreover, the experience we have of God is often mingled with the sense of our own sinfulness, with the experience of what Scripture calls "God's wrath." Again, the experience of the creator's love often seems to be contradicted by others of a wholly contrary kind, such as the sense of being engulfed by the incomprehensible, or of being rejected in the finiteness, the wretchedness, the bitterness of death—the experience of the "death" of God.

Whatever may be the nature of our experience of the Mystery, we should never take it as the norm of the only experience wholly "commensurate" with the absolute Mystery. Thus we should not declare that an experience would not allow "God" to be God if it were felt as the sense of his nearness, as the desire to address him trustfully as Thou and to speak to him. To declare apriori that looking for God's loving nearness is altogether senseless and childishly arrogant shows that one does not really consider God as a person.

A man who claims that he has a "lofty" concept of God may well have measured him with a yardstick of his own in which there is a direct correspondence between "submissiveness" and "remoteness," while "sublimity" and "intimacy" are inversely related. What shall we think of one who believes that deep down in his being he has by subjective implication the "transcendental" experience of the fact that the supreme

Mystery is the mystery of the utter nearness of intimate love and not only of the aloof remoteness of God in his silent sublimity? It is unnecessary that *everyone* should achieve this experience before it can be accepted as valid. It is required even less that everybody should be able to make the experience of such a subjectively transcendental implication clearly and distinctly explicit.

Would it be folly to rely in this matter on another person's experience and with this other to adore the Mystery as one of loving intimacy? Especially if the other were able to vindicate his experience by proofs we need not consider here? After all, it is obvious that every experience presupposes a certain capacity, and hence not all people have the same experiences, with the same range and intensity. Not everybody has a feeling for music. It would be unwise for one who has never had the "experience of Bach" to deny that others may have it, for this would mean giving the same weight to the lack of an experience as to the experience itself. We should not equate the experience of darkness with that of light. Likewise we should not exaggerate the validity of the experience of remoteness, as if it would of itself exclude any possibility of the experience of a free, total nearness of God in grace. Actually the two experiences are not mutually exclusive. The experience of such nearness presupposes, on the contrary, a sense of God's remoteness, since one who becomes aware of him as near at hand is conscious that this is a marvel of his love, not something he himself could merit or bring about. Hence God is experienced as one who but for this marvel would be at an immense distance. And *at least* in the experience of God's nearness as an *undeserved* favor there is contained implicitly the knowledge of the possibility of his remoteness, overcome always only by him. We may also say: the possibility of a relationship is not excluded by the fact that it does not exist; but the *free* relationship in love provides experiential proof that there might not be any relationship at all.

Is it possible to have a relationship with God as the incomprehensible mystery? We can only ask the sceptic once more whether the lack of personal evidence outweighs the evidence of someone else—whether it can invalidate the personal experience of another. All are capable of scepticism, but not all succeed in lifting up their voices in the darkness (for even in this intimacy darkness remains), and not everyone is capable of conceiving of himself as one to whom God is communicating himself, or might communicate himself. It is so much easier to think of oneself as small, insignificant, a nothing! It is not only easier, it is safer—safer, at any rate, than to believe in the possibility of a God near at hand. For if we exclude this possibility, if we let the mystery remain the mystery in the distance or even the mystery lying beyond every attainable experience, it also remains beyond the possibility of making any claims on man. This means that God becomes unimportant, harmless; that the problems and the risks of the domain of metaphysics are no longer man's concern, they are beyond his reach; God is "too high," and rises ever higher, until in the end he becomes a very thin sort of reality and very innocuous. Then man reaches the point where he must no longer try to live with infinity—it would only send him into a daze—where the uncanny mysteriousness has given way and the mystery is no longer mystery. Then man retreats into finiteness as into a shelter where "the mystery" can no longer harm him.

The experience of the mystery cannot be put into words and

"taught" to any man. But he can be helped to experience it:
in his freedom, as he ventures trustfully into the incomprehensible; in his anxiety, his joy; in experiences he might not
have explicitly noted owing to their "mysteriousness," which
might be lost to him because he did not take them seriously
enough, which might also have embittered him, because in
them the mystery came too near. He may interpret what others
have gone through in the light of what he himself has experienced. After all, no one should imagine that his own horizon
is the ultimate boundary. It has always been considered wise
to learn from the experience of others, in the field of religion
as well as in other domains. It is a fact that man stands in
open communication with his fellow men. He may be unique
and irreplaceable, yet, in the final analysis, he remains only
one among many. As an individual he can never wholly and
at once realize the range of possibilities which stand open for
man as such. Since a man always lives in communion with
others, it would amount to a denial of part of his existence if
he refused to learn from them, to try to see through them what
he himself may have overlooked. Also, the other person might
be braver than he. Personally one might perhaps ascribe what
one feels to the influence of character, ability, the weather,
hormones—anything, rather than to the impact of the mystery.
It is possible that the other person understands what one does
not understand oneself. At any rate, as a mere individual, man
remains a tributary of mankind as a whole, which can realize
as a whole what is always given to the individual only as a
never totally fulfilled possibility within the range of his possibilities. That is, in the individual it is given only partially,
while in humanity as a whole it is present in an infinitely more
intensive, concentrated and suggestive manner.

If we look at the experience of mankind in its history, at the history of its religious development, we are clearly told that man has the experience of the Incomprehensible. This incomprehensible something does not merely disturb and evoke dread, it is also felt as a power which loves man and welcomes him. We may call this experience "mysticism" or "devotion" or an encounter with the Holy, we may speak of the numinous or of the wholly other, or of that which differs radically from all the rest, the "night" or the "light." None of these terms touch the innermost nature of this religious phenomenon, which remains the same even when the different religions use the most diverse categorical systems to express it and to render it in the most diverse metaphysical and theoretical translations. And even if these translations contradict each other (as a rule, they merely seem to); even if they did contradict each other really, and if their formulation were ever so bizarre (we might almost say, ever so tasteless), that which stands behind all this and manifests itself in all this remains throughout: the experience of *the* mystery.

5 / The Implication of the Mystery as Faith

To believe means in its derivation to approve, to consent, to accept something in freedom, to say Yes to it. In the act of real faith we say Yes to what the other person states, we accept it not because we see ourselves that it is so, for reasons based on our own insight. Rather the consent is given in the trustful knowledge that the other person is reliable, worthy of faith. Faith which is not "blind," not contrary to reason, implies a relation of confidence, of sympathy for the other. It implies also the readiness to enter into what the other says, in such a way that, while "listening" to him, we give him the opportunity of giving, as it were, a proof that he deserves to be believed, of showing himself to us who believe in him as a person who is worthy of our faith. Where there is faith, two persons grow closer to each other, there is an increasing familiarity and intimacy between them.

All this likewise applies to our faith in "God." It is not our intention here to explain the whole nature of this faith, with its attentive listening to God and to his self-manifestation. We propose to study only one of its basic elements, one of the roots of faith, the root which is or can be present in the very act of existing and which God's elevating grace can, in the concrete order of salvation, make into something more than a mere element, can transform into the whole faith itself.

This root of faith, which under the influence of God's grace turns into a real, although perhaps only subjectively implicit, faith is man's primordial confidence in the meaning of existence. We may at once call it simply "faith," not a faith which man actually "possesses" but a faith which "happens." It happens like one's faith in a person, on the basis of confidence, of readiness to pay attention, to listen (listening means both: hearing and obeying), thus giving the other person, in this case God, the opportunity to come nearer, to be the one who gives an answer, while man himself is the one who is vitally interested in such an answer, for reasons involving both his mind and his existence. For faith is not only a matter of the intellect; as an act of religion it involves the whole of man, it concerns all the dimensions of his existence, it affects his existence as such. Hence faith is always present where one lives one's life, lives it in such a way that one accepts it, consents to it, welcomes it. This welcoming does not take place "blindly," without any reason, but on the basis of that primordial confidence which makes one believe in the meaningfulness of existence, thus inducing one to accept in advance all the unforeseeable and unavoidable turns that life will take.

If this acquiescence is not to be unreasonable, then what is not previsible and avoidable cannot simply be something which just happens, fortuitously, by chance; it must be something in relation to which man stands in open readiness. It is as when a person trusts the darkness of a room. Although it is dark and he actually sees nothing, he nonetheless "sees" that the room is not empty. The darkness is not for him mere obscurity, something negative, yielding nothing. It yields something, but only to one who enters it with readiness to accept what it conceals.

The same thing applies to the unforeseeable in life; life also gives something only to one who trusts what it has in store. It gives this as something concealed, with the expectation that it will be accepted as such. Likewise people who love each other expect that each will accept something from the other, without really knowing what it is he accepts.

They do of course expect from each other an effort at understanding. As people stand in relation to each other, so they stand before their unfathomable existence: they are convinced in advance that *ultimately* they will never understand it, but must accept the unfathomable as unfathomable; or rather that, if it is accepted as that which is *at first* the unfathomable, *it* turns into something meaningful, sheltering, something infinitely rich and spacious. They realize that this "ultimate" reality is not to be measured by a yardstick of their own, that they must yield to it as that which has the last word.

How can man live his life without despairing, except with such a faith? Without despairing about the fact that, although he is free and aware of it, he can never really feel "free"? True, he has the freedom to decide for or against something, to say Yes or No. But he is not free to say neither. And whether he says Yes or No, in any event he "commits" himself to something he cannot take in in a glance, whose consequences he cannot fully foresee, at the moment of his decision. For this decision always applies to some "material" cast up before him which he does not totally understand.

We never really foresee how things to which we now say Yes or No will develop in the future, yet we must make a choice. Such a choice leads to despair unless we realize that the unfathomable and the uncontrollable are "existential features" of our life; unless, in accepting them, we make of this basic confidence, which is a full trust in the mystery as such and in the way it directs our life, the foundation of our activity and of our every decision. This fundamental confidence is more than resignation. It is a kind of open simplicity untroubled by the fact that there is no absolute point of vantage from which we can arrange our spiritual existence in an autonomous way; it acquiesces in the fact that, although free and autonomous, we remain forever creatures whose life is not planned by themselves, who, from the moment of their birth, already incline in a certain direction. The possible courses always pre-exist our free decision, the "materials" of our choice are there before we decide about them.

Such is the basic nature of man. On the one hand he is free; on the other hand, he is subject to a pre-established directionallty in his existence. He *may* choose between Yes or No, and he *must* make the choice. Therefore he can come to terms with life without despair only if his basic option is for this fundamental confidence by which he tells himself: whatever happens, and in whatever manner, a man must put the final— the very final—responsibility for the success, or—if that is the way things look—for the failure of his life, not in himself but in something which controls him and which he cannot himself control; in something he can neither predict nor fathom, through which he relies on the inscrutable, with which he is involved as with the incalculable, a hidden factor in his every undertaking. For every human activity precontains incalculable, unforeseeable, uncontrollable elements which cannot be taken into account, concerning which man never knows whether or not they will upset what he has planned, so that, in the last analysis—it sometimes seems to him—everything issues not in sense but in nonsense. True, we are wont to say that an action carried out freely and responsibly, undertaken only after we have weighed the different possibilities and reached a reasonable decision—that such an action is of itself meaningful. Otherwise it would not be an action planned in freedom and responsibility after an objective examination of the given state of affairs. Even if we forget that refusing to act is also a decision—although generally we believe that through such a refusal we may escape the responsibility for a decision left in abeyance—how can we ever reach an "objective" decision? Of course we must "objectively" examine the situation in order to be able to justify our decision. But when we have really weighed the motives for or against an action—insofar as they can be reflectively known in the given situation—are we certain then that we act "objectively"? If and insofar as "objectively" means "in an objectivated manner"—that is, in an express, explicit manner—there is no adequate objectivation in the planning of a decision. Unavoidably man acts out of motives he can never render wholly explicit. For, not to mention other reasons, reflecting on one's motives again occurs as a free action, that is under the influence of motives, drives and horizons which would also stand in need of analysis and investigation. Reflection never wholly catches up with freedom, never entirely elaborates the materials of freedom and their original motivation.

Hence no point of view exists which is based on total reflection. For the justification of our single actions this means that man does more things than he can justify in an "objectivistic" manner. One who wished to make sure, in a reflectively adequate way, of the rightness of his actions would never be able to initiate any act, he would lapse into the spiritual neurosis of scrupulosity—which is the punishment of that hidden pride whereby man wants to steer his own course and will not entrust himself, without worry or fear, to another being, to the Uncontrollable, to the Mystery and the Judgment of his existence. Since man's responsibility sees only the beginning, never the end, it does not grasp the nature of what it is willing to assume. And so it is with freedom. Man wants to do only what he sees clearly as in accordance with his will. A day comes when he finds out that he has acted freely in a way not in accord with what he willed or with the responsibility he had assumed. True, we may rightly reply that we are *responsible* in our freedom only for what we foresee and decide in advance. That which actually follows on our decisions may be painful and tragic, but it does not affect our moral personality. It would be foolish and neurotic to carry the harsh burden of responsibility for what has been set in motion involuntarily, although many people feel as their own guilt that which is merely chance or the shortsightedness of a finite being. But we have already said that there are motives we have freely chosen, for which we are responsible, and which do *not* come under our reflexive deliberation. Freedom and reflexively objectivated freedom are not the same thing. Hence that person is right, shows greater wisdom and insight, who considers the possibility, without apodictically asserting it as a fact, that in the objective wrongness of his decision he encounters, deep down in his primordial unreflective freedom, the objectivation of motives which he has freely chosen and for which he really remains responsible.

It is precisely for this reason that reflexive computation

never catches up with our freedom or responsibility, and the experience of being unable to find out where we stand—even as a free and responsible person—is not a symptom of scrupulosity and neurotic anxiety. It corresponds to reality as long as man does not have the courage to entrust himself and his unreflective "morality" to the uncontrollable Mystery whose name is God.

Faith in life? If it is true that every action involves a reality man does not grasp or comprehend, we can really say: faith in life means: accepting the incomprehensible as such, accepting it with that basic confidence which does not try to reach total reflexive clarity from the start; which, although it does reflect, knows that ultimately things make sense and that there is in the heart of existence a power which pardons and heals. Because of this power life is not heading nowhere, the final issue is not meaninglessness but sense. This act of faith, this experiential relation to God, means that one lives one's life without anxiety, something which calls for the utmost exertion of heart and spirit. Man is not always up to such an effort. When he is tired and without hope, sinking and drowning in his finiteness, he is unable to realize what he already knows as a matter of experience: that ultimate reality supports and shelters us and does not expose us to the whims of chance; that it forbears and forgives, rather than sitting in stern judgment on us; that it welcomes us with love rather than plunging us into the nothingness of our limitations.

At the beginning of this chapter we noted that this basic confidence in the meaningfulness of our uncontrollable existence is not only an essential root of faith, but in the actual order of salvation is more than that, although not of itself alone; namely, that it is already faith in the proper theological sense of the word, even though only subjectively implicit faith.

Why is this so? Our answer is addressed first to the Christian and starts, as we have said, from his premises. Whether, and to what extent, a non-Christian—that is, an "anonymous" Christian—can understand it is another question. First, through basic confidence man makes up his mind to accept the unfathomable and the uncontrollable, hence the mystery as such, as it is in itself and as it holds sway over us. Since the mystery as such is present and is accepted, even though at times only in a subjectively implicit manner, the uncontrollable is not simply a minus quantity, something wholly unknown which one cannot get excited about. It is something one accepts. In this basic confidence God is accepted as he is precisely in those features which we do not understand. But this implies that moral characteristic which constitutes the dignity of faith proper: humble acquiescence in a supreme rule which is no longer one's own. Moreover, this acquiescence may, in a subjectively implicit way, be held in being by what we call grace.

This is what we mean. The basic acquiescence in existence is ontologically raised by grace—that is, ultimately by God himself. This transforms its transcendental horizon. The self-communication of God as the Mystery is experienced in absolute proximity (when this growing proximity is accepted), even if only in subjective implication which may never be made reflectively explicit. And this may be considered as a "revelation" of God to man, so that man's affirmative answer to it is "faith" in the proper sense of the word. We do not say that the basic confidence is, of itself, already such a faith. But when it is raised and divinized through grace, because of God's salvific will, it contains what may be accepted in true faith, the revealing self-communication of God. It may not yet be translated through reflection into human words. Of himself the man may be unable to do this. Only the Christian may be capable of interpreting basic confidence with its subjective implication in this way, *after* he has expressly heard in the official message of revelation what superhuman marvels are wrought deep down in man by grace and the action of God. But all this does not take away from what we may say: basic confidence, where it is actually present, is more than itself, it is subjectively implicit faith.

Why should basic confidence not be called "faith" when, at the foundation of his existence, man senses that the absolute Mystery is not high and remote but is totally near, permeating his existence and giving him the courage to believe that his "secret"—that is, uncleansed—guilt has been forgiven? We may call this experience the "private" self-attestation and self-communication of God, yet it occurs also in, and on account of, Christ. It is impossible to deny that man undergoes this experience, even if in the unreflective depths of his being and of his free activity. In one who receives a divine self-communication and self-revelation directly, the docile acceptance of it is called faith. Hence faith is not something opposed to the experience described above, it is the positive response to it. This experience derives from the free self-manifestation of God, since the experienced proximity and forgiveness are his gifts. Therefore basic confidence, raised and divinized by God's grace, can be more than it might be by itself alone; it can be real faith in God, in his close proximity and his forgiveness. The docile acquiescence in life contains (or better, may contain) the obedience of faith itself, because God freely gives himself to this life. As a rule this may be known *explicitly* only by a Christian. Many non-Christians will make this act of faith only in subjective implication. All men *can* make it, because deep down in their being God's grace is extended to all, and *when* they do in fact accept their lives in real obedience, God's grace turns their docility into a real faith.

The insight we have thus reached that there may be faith in the divine self-revelation even when there is no faith in the proper theological sense of the word needs further clarification. This will unavoidably entail a few repetitions.

Man is necessarily involved with "God." In everything that he comprehends, he encounters the incomprehensible. We might say that he lives in association with this incomprehensible, unfathomable, uncontrollable, unpredictable "Mystery." He may welcome this reality which he can not grasp or understand or really know, he may also reject it. Expressly or implicitly, this is, at any rate, man's fundamental position: he stands open to God, he experiences God, he is a "theist," and he is such necessarily.

We said that man is a theist. But this does not take us far, since it is the anonymous *Christian* we are interested in. To be a Christian, more is required than the metaphysically necessary ordination towards the absolute being, truth, the "mystery" of the unfathomable. Man does not reach his salvation as a metaphysician, as an anonymous metaphysical theist. He reaches it only because, and insofar as, he possesses "faith," specifically *Christian* faith, a faith which is not a knowledge of God's existence reached by man autonomously through metaphysical insight but a free assent to a spoken divine revelation in which God himself addresses man and communicates himself to him. It is a communication accepted as truth *because of* the authority of the God who reveals himself, and not on the basis of a metaphysical insight concerning this truth on man's part. Man reaches his salvation through faith understood in this sense, and only through it. Theology speaks of faith as of the "means necessary for salvation," calling it necessary as a means because, as a beginning of salvation, it is already a sharing of God's truth, cannot be replaced by anything else, is the indispensable means on which salvation depends even when, with no guilt on man's part involved, it seems not to be available to him.

Besides this necessity as a means (*necessitas medii*), there is also the *necessitas praecepti,* the necessity deriving from a precept. Here we have a law on whose fulfillment God makes man's salvation depend, but which benefits or hinders salvation only if and insofar as man knows of this law, consciously and freely accepts or rejects it. This second kind of necessity comes exclusively from the fact that God has given this precept. Because and insofar as he has given it, man is obliged to do what is required if he wishes to reach salvation. But he can obey an order only if he knows of it. If he does not know of it—and all the more if he is unable to learn of it—he can neither obey it nor, should he disobey it, be liable to punishment. It would be unjust to make salvation depend on the fulfillment of a commandment when this lies beyond a human being's powers. Suppose that salvation should depend on a prescribed pilgrimage to Rome. In this case God could not in justice deny beatitude to somebody who had not made the pilgrimage, either because he was unaware of this condition or was for some reason, physical or other, unable to fulfill it. Otherwise we should have to say that (possibly because it is wholly gratuitous) God might, and in fact does, deny salvation for no reason, since he would certainly not be showing any real will for the salvation of the person in question. It follows that there are cases where a distinction may be made between an obligation deriving from a precept and salvation itself, which is linked up with the fulfillment of this precept through legislation of some kind. This distinction is possible because salvation, the goal to be reached, is not really brought about by the thing prescribed but is only connected with it as with an exterior condition. It is a wholly different matter, as we have said, when what is involved is necessary for salvation as a means. Even when a man is unaware of this means through no fault of his own, he cannot reach salvation, the goal, because the "means" as such is a constitutive element of the goal; the goal depends on this means for its very existence.

Theology further distinguishes means which are absolutely necessary and means which are hypothetically necessary for salvation. Thus sacramental baptism is hypothetically necessary for salvation, but we say that in case of need it can be replaced by other means—a certain attitude, a certain subjective disposition or decision. A means which is absolutely necessary, on the other hand, can be replaced by nothing; faith and love cannot be replaced, salvation depends absolutely on them, since it is brought about by them. For "salvation" means love for God which has become definitive. If this love is to issue in eternity, man must practice it in time, during his life. Only thus can he possess God. But this doctrine of the absolute necessity of certain means for salvation brings up a difficulty. We take God's *universal* salvific will for granted, we believe that God truly and seriously entertains it. We believe that God gives to all men, at all times, in all places, under all circumstances the necessary means to reach salvation. If, then, faith is a necessary means of salvation, this implies, in the hypothesis of the universal salvific will, that God gives each man the possibility of having this faith.

On the other hand, we say that faith is present only when it is based upon, and is a response to, God's revelation, which man perceives as "spoken revelation." Therefore, if God wills salvation for all and wishes to offer every man what is required for it, he must see to it that everyone can in fact hear his revealing word. But can everyone really hear it? St. Paul says: "How are they to hear if no one preaches?" (Rom. 10:14). Do all men hear such preaching? Historical experience shows, at any rate, that throughout countless centuries there have been innumerable multitudes of men (and there still are) who have been reached neither by the revelation of the Old Testament nor the revelation in Jesus Christ, men whom the Church too does not reach, and obviously without any guilt of their own. Thus, apparently, it is a matter of experience that God does not make faith a possibility for these men. So we stand again before the dilemma presented in the first chapter: either God does not have a universal salvific will, or faith is not the means necessary for salvation. It is precisely this riddle which seems to confront us when we claim that there are anonymous Christians. For this implies that there are people who believe in Christ without knowing that they do; they do not know it mainly because they have not come sufficiently into contact with divine revelation. But how can they believe in Christ in this case? Is this theologically possible?

If we wish to show that it is possible we must enter into a discussion with theology itself by trying to establish the convergence, actual or possible, between explicit and implicit Christianity, between faith in life and reflective, thematic faith with an explicit conceptualized content, stated in propositions; between the relation with God as experienced in life and that which historical Christianity teaches explicitly.

But theology itself, even if it should not hold all that we hold—that is, if it were unwilling to admit the existence of implicit anonymous Christianity and Christian salvific faith—faces the same dilemma. For it affirms as unconditional the universal salvific will of God and as equally unconditional the necessity of a Christian faith which can be replaced by nothing else.

Let us first see how theology tries to get out of this quandary. We shall proceed schematically, that is, summarize what it has to say in this matter under four "possible solutions." This does not mean that there are four clearly distinct solutions and that we would have to decide which one comes nearest to solving the problem. On the contrary, the four may exist simultaneously, as theoretical possibilities, and if we tie our own considerations in with them, this should not be understood as if each solution totally excluded all the others.

The *first* solution proposed involves the existence of a primitive revelation and holds that every human being comes into relation with it, even though it may be in a very unthematic way. It maintains, therefore, that everywhere, in all parts of the earth, possibly as the tribal traditions of a people, there are elements transmitted from the origins of mankind as divine revelation, not merely as *human* tradition. Let us suppose that man says "Yes" to the contents which have been transmitted in this way: he would then make a real act of faith, and he would make it because of the authority of God manifesting himself.

The theory does not have to hold that this tradition should

necessarily reach each individual man. Much would already be gained if we might suppose that this primitive tradition would have reached many men, at least in the early history of mankind. In this view, what has been transmitted from Adam need no longer be so important for modern man. One who hears the revelation spoken in Jesus Christ and has access also to the Old Testament, and welcomes in faith the God who reveals himself in them, stands in no need of a primitive revelation orally transmitted. But for early times, and for considerable segments of humanity during these early times, this hypothetical primitive revelation might be quite essential.

There are also, however, considerable difficulties against this theory. First, the time element. Fifty or a hundred years ago no one had any idea of it, people spoke of a pre-historical period of a few thousand, or at the most ten thousand, years. Today not only paleontologists, but theologians too, know that this time may well amount to a million years. It is difficult to imagine that the primitive revelation should have been transmitted over such a long stretch of time even if we may take it for granted that throughout history man lives from tradition in this sense at least, that there is no human being who begins from the beginning, who is not heir to the experience, the customs, the way of life of previous generations, even when, as a "revolutionary," he rebels against them. (See what we said above on implication in tradition.)

But even if we assumed the absolute necessity and real existence of a tradition which, to some extent, reached every man, this would not take care of all difficulties. We would not yet have established that this tradition transmitted a *divine* revelation. Even if we could show that man respected and obeyed it (as something handed down in history), this would not yet imply that it was the tradition of the word spoken by *God* at the beginning of time.

Paleontology might add another difficulty. All we have discovered about the earliest man—even when he can be considered metaphysically a real man, that is, a spiritual, thinking being—shows him to have been at so low a cultural level that he can hardly be thought of as the bearer of a primordial tradition. He cannot either have been the vehicle of this tradition or have passed it on—at least if we conceive it, as is usually done, as expressed in ideas and statements and transmitted in *this* form. If, on the other hand, overlooking Adam in Paradise, we conceive this tradition as a "transcendental" result of grace itself, we come back to the revelation in subjective implication already discussed. In this hypothesis there is no longer any need to postulate a primordial revelation to provide for the faith of subsequent generations. When we say that the earliest man could hardly be considered as a bearer of primordial tradition, we should be careful to note that these men who are poised on the hypothetical line of demarcation between "biosphere" and "noosphere" and are really human, are not to be compared with what we call the primitive peoples of our time. For the latter are already in possession of a remarkable system of ethics, of very respectable tribal traditions and initiation rites. They are not primitive in the sense in which we apply the term to the men at the dawn of history.

A *second* suggested solution postulates a special illumination, some kind of "private revelation" which God would provide for those not reached by his historic, universal, official revelation. This second theory holds that after, perhaps, a primordial revelation, human beings in general are reached by the historic revelation of the Old Testament or of Jesus Christ, through the official, or at least the public, universal revelation. But it is undeniable that in many cases this seems difficult to establish. In such "exceptional cases," therefore, it is proposed, God makes up for the absence of the universal historic revelation by means of some kind of private revelation, a special illumination resembling—at least in a rudimentary way—that which takes place in the prophets. God communicates himself to the prophets for themselves and for others. They pass on this divine communication as a message from God.

It is difficult to deny the basic possibility of such a communication once one has accepted the possibility of a divine revelation to man. St. Thomas was already wondering how a man "who grows up in the woods," a completely "wild" man, could meet revelation. He too admits that for such a "wild" individual an act of faith may become possible through a special revelation. But this theory becomes difficult to accept when we are no longer dealing with exceptional cases. Unlike the older thinkers, we are aware of how incredibly long and far-flung the history of mankind is, and we must certainly admit that more than a few individual instances are involved. We can no longer assert, with the Fathers of the Church and the theologians of the Middle Ages, that the Christian or the Old Testament history of revelation has reached all, with relatively rare exceptions. They took it for granted that mankind did not go back very far beyond Moses and Abraham; God had also spoken to the patriarchs before Abraham; mankind as a whole had existed for from 4000 to 6000 years, and more or less exclusively around the Mediterranean sea. Since all this can no longer be accepted, the "theory of exceptions" has lost much of its weight. For, we might argue, since God inevitably *does* send his revelation to so many human beings in a peculiar way, why then does he not simply let this be the way of manifesting himself to mankind at large? Why must there still be a real, historical official revelation?

The *third* solution suggested insists upon the conditional nature of the universal salvific will of God. It is conditional in this sense, that the doctrine of the *universal* salvific will contains no necessary implication that God does, in fact, save *all* men. He provides all men with a sufficient opportunity to decide freely in favor of him and to reach salvation. We must remember that many men, by sinning against the *natural* law —and hence through their own fault—have shown themselves unworthy of the further supernatural help of a private revelation and of supernatural grace within them. Revelation is never extended to such individuals. Like those of St. Augustine and of Jansenism this theory harbors a pessimistic view of the general moral standing of mankind. For it, mankind is so wretched —wretched even in the sight of God—that not only in a few individual cases but in vast numbers, and not only objectively but also subjectively, God's will is so grievously transgressed that, despite his universal salvific will, he is finally relieved of any obligation, as it were, to pursue such a wicked creature with his revelation. Man has from the start shown himself unworthy of such special solicitude on the part of God. And the theory concludes that, inasmuch as countless men, maybe the majority, have made themselves unworthy of this divine concern through their own guilt, it is no argument against the universal salvific will of God if revelation does not reach them.

It cannot be denied apriori that concrete individual instances of an absence of contact with revelation and of the loss of salvation may be explained in this manner, despite God's universal conditional salvific will. For when someone sins grievously against the essential laws of his human nature, he must not be surprised if, within this order of nature thus defiled by sin, revelation too is lacking. Neither should anybody expect a private message from God if he does not attend to Christian revelation owing to his own culpable spiritual indolence. It cannot be denied that man may sin indirectly even against faith or the possibility of faith. But this by no means vindicates a theory which burdens the *majority* of mankind, subjectively, with such a weight of guilt as would justify God's providence in denying his revelation in fact to an immense portion of mankind despite his universal salvific will. Indeed it always remains an open question whether, and to what extent, humanity as a whole, in all its objective transgressions against God's law, is subjectively guilty as well. Even if one gives an optimistic answer to this question, as everyone is entitled to do, it does not in the least follow that one finds reasons for rejoicing in the course of history and in mankind's moral situation. But who is going to decide whether this state of mankind involves guilt rather than misfortune, whether this world history with all its depravity is not a record of finiteness and stupidity more than one of guilt? With all its objective culpability it may be interpreted as a history of unavoidable "crises of development," of groping and fumbling, rather than as one of a subjective guilt incurring divine condemnation (although the fact of judgment, too, undoubtedly remains). Thus it might contain an occasion for divine forbearance and mercy, rather than be the grounds for God's denial, to a great segment of this race of man, of his revelation as a prerequisite of salvation. Otherwise God would not earnestly will the salvation of *this* concrete humanity—something which we cannot say without heresy.

If we consider this alleged universal subjective guilt, something more argues against this theory. Christianity makes it clear that it is precisely to the *sinner* that God offers a revelation unto salvation. The salvific will goes out to sinners, not to those who observe the natural moral law on the level of nature, and who would be rewarded for this by a supernatural revelation. The universal salvific will is rightly understood only when it means the salvation of those men also who have incurred subjective guilt, when it makes faith possible for the sinner. True, it is theoretically possible that in individual cases God might at first extend only a remote possibility of belief and, if man should reject it, refuse the proximate possibility. And this remote possibility might consist in the fact that, through his grace, God enables man to fulfill the natural moral law and thus sets in motion a development leading all the way up to faith, provided man does not fail from the beginning of this divine process of education. But even should we admit this, we are not entitled to generalize and to say that since most men are sinners they have not the concrete possibility of finding the faith. For this would imply a denial that salvation is proffered to the sinner. Let us remember that salvation and faith are the same thing; otherwise we could not speak of the necessity of faith for salvation. Therefore, when God offers salvation to man, to sinful man—precisely to him—he offers him faith, real faith. Hence we reject as a possible solution of our problem the theory that because of man's sin God refuses to invite him immediately through revelation.

The *fourth* proposed solution is the doctrine of so-called virtual faith. This faith is called "virtual" in contrast to "formal" faith—that is, the assent to God's testimony as really offered and really heard. It is a moral attitude which may be considered equivalent to formal faith and contains within itself the power and the readiness (*virtus*) for formal faith. The theory of virtual faith comes from the theologian Anton Straub. About fifty years ago he suggested that when revelation does not reach man—without any guilt of his own—God might accept as salvific, instead of the faith in which something is believed, a mere readiness to believe, an attitude of willingness to believe. This readiness to believe is salvific inasmuch as one who is willing to believe stands before God as one who listens, who obeys, who fundamentally submits to the authority of the God of truth and thus displays an attitude which, from the moral and personal point of view, is equivalent to real listening and believing and to actual assent. In case of necessity this might be sufficient. The fact is, says Straub, that we can hardly conceive how God's revelation could have reached countless men of earlier times and cultures outside the West. But as they had acknowledged God with their natural reason, they might have stood before him with such a readiness to believe and to obey, with an inner disposition to receive from God the ultimate principles of life. Although such men did not possess formal faith, they lived in a basic disposition which was tantamount to faith.

We should not confuse Straub's ideas with a theory, condemned in the eighteenth century, that, if need be, a metaphysical knowledge of God is sufficient. Straub does not say this. He does not claim that man has virtual faith sufficient for salvation when he acknowledges God with the help of natural reason and, drawing the moral consequences from this knowledge, observes the natural law. He says only this: there is an authentic inner readiness to believe deriving, with the help of grace, from man's natural power of knowledge. This readiness to believe, which may be present before revelation is actually heard, is a substitute for formal faith in the proper sense. These ideas of Straub, although not often mentioned, have not wholly disappeared. The magisterium of the Church has not rejected them.

But we might object that Straub defines as the requisite for salvation, the "means" as such, something which only resembles faith—the readiness to assent should God reveal himself. And even if we accept this theory as valid only in cases of necessity, it seems very difficult to reconcile it with the requirement of the Church of a faith in which something is believed. For this theory, salvation would come from an attitude on man's part, not from the reality of God imparted to man in the word of God.

So much for the four "attempted solutions"—attempted insofar as they are efforts to reconcile the evidence from the history of the world and of religion that the majority of mankind does not have the faith, with the universal salvific will of God, a will which seems to carry with it the implications at least that man has a possibility of hearing the word of revelation.

We would like to offer some comments on these four proposed solutions. First, what about a primitive tradition? Suppose that we could show that everywhere on earth, whether in China, India, Patagonia, people know that the Pythagorean theorem is true and why it is true. Would we say then that such knowledge is present only because this theorem had been passed along through tradition? Should we not rather say that the mathematical knowledge which is the basis for this theorem is so self-evident that everybody has it, that everybody understands the theorem, that everybody at once and everywhere discovers it, or can discover it, for himself? True, at some time and somewhere somebody has been the first to discover it, and he has also transmitted it. Many people would never discover it if they were not led by some doctrinal tradition to examine it and to discover its truth anew for themselves. However, this does not take away from the fact that it is constantly discovered anew. Such is the case with the Pythagorean theorem.

Applying this mixture and mutual interaction of originality and tradition to our own problem, we might say: "God" is continually discovered anew. It is true that our first ancestors "discovered" him originally, and what they discovered, they also transmitted as primitive revelation. But this experience is of such a nature that it is an obvious one for everybody—even if only in a homeopathic dose—that everyone has, or can have, it afresh. In the same manner we understand Pythagoras and we even "discover" his theorem, yet we would not have discovered it on our own if somebody had not "induced" us to do so. Hence there is no basic contradiction between the role of tradition and the dawning of a new idea, the transmission of a truth and the fact that it is spontaneously discovered in concrete life. And so it may happen that we discover a proposition *because* it has been transmitted. On the other hand, the tradition may stay alive *because* the proposition can ever be discovered anew. Tradition and man's own creative knowledge sustain and influence each other, each presupposes the other. The simplest illustration of this may be found in language. Few ideas would be discovered if they were not already embedded in transmitted language and supplied by it. Men would not advert to them if they did not already have the words for this purpose. But the opposite is also true: men would forget most words if they did not come up against them in the very things these words designated.

A mutual interaction of this kind between tradition and personal knowledge or experience occurs not only between human tradition, on the one hand, and a merely natural knowledge, on the other, but also between divine tradition and man's knowledge of God as inspired by grace. Several combinations are possible. Thus a human tradition may later have been incorporated in a divine revelation. An earlier divine tradition may have been passed along as natural knowledge. A purely human tradition may have been taken up by a later, purely natural knowledge. A divine tradition may have been assumed by a later more explicit revelation of God. All these combinations are at least possible.

In the light of these general, more abstract, considerations we may say: if we admit the reality of a primitive revelation, many of its data may be transmitted because they are also objects of natural knowledge. If the first men knew through a primitive revelation of God that a living, personal God existed, they may have passed this truth on. And such a transmission can easily keep going on, because it concerns a truth which can always be rediscovered through natural knowledge. On the other hand, this natural knowledge which can be constantly rediscovered may always have re-emerged because it is also part of the data of God's transmitted revelation. Moreover, it may happen that such a truth, coming originally from revelation, precisely because it can also be reached by simple natural knowledge, comes gradually to be transmitted more as a mere human tradition or as spontaneous natural knowledge which man can constantly rediscover, like the Pythagorean theorem. This would mean that the revealed

character of such a truth would be lost in a knowledge which
is a merely metaphysical and natural knowledge of God.
Gradually, tradition as such, purely as such, would cease to
afford the occasion of a real assent of faith, because a real
assent of faith is based on the revealed character of a statement, not on the possibility of its verification as natural knowledge. But even granted this—it is precisely the objection we
made to the theory of a primitive revelation—we should keep
in mind that the knowledge of such a transmitted truth, even
of one which can be the object of natural knowledge, is constantly raised, sustained, and as it were encompassed, by
divine grace.[1] It follows that even if tradition supplies to man
a religious moral truth which seems to be merely one of the
natural order, nevertheless the hearing and accepting of this
truth, insofar as it happens in the light of grace, may have the
character of an assent of faith, of an act of faith. On the
other hand, since this religious truth, although knowable naturally, is passed along in tradition, divine grace, insofar as it
makes the assent of faith possible, has a point of contact in
the human being. For, should nothing have been transmitted,
even this point of contact would be lacking. Humanly speaking, divine grace would find it much harder to effect "something" in man and to offer a merely natural truth within a
horizon projected by grace itself in such a way that the assent
to this truth would really assume the quality of faith. Hence
we may say: of itself primitive tradition cannot bring about
the quality of an assent in faith to a divine revelation as such,
because in the course of time an explicit tradition of the revealed character of this truth is lost, or is not kept alive with
sufficient clarity. Nevertheless this theory of a primitive tradi-

[1] Cp. pp. 96ff. "The second premise. . . ."

tion contains a really meaningful element, provided we link it up with the doctrine that man is always "moved" and sustained by divine grace. We still have to show that the opinion that man's spiritual existence is always sustained and wholly encompassed by grace can be considered a datum of revelation. This brings us back more explicitly to the considerations which are essential for our whole problem.

We start from the statement: the universal history of salvation is also always fundamentally a universal history of revelation. This statement refers first and mainly to theology. In order to give a theological justification of it, we shall mention a few premises which may be considered as common and generally accepted doctrine within Catholic theology.

The *first* premise: the universal salvific will of God, from which it follows that God offers his supernatural grace to all men. This means that every man is given what we call supernatural grace required for salvation. It may be given as proffered grace, as *gratia praeveniens,* a prevenient, actual impulse given to man's freedom; or it may be given as accepted, welcomed grace, to which man consents. This is a premise which, obviously, the so-called pagan neither understands nor accepts. But this does not matter in the present stage of our considerations. We only wish now to point out to the theologian that on the basis of his own premises, without detracting from the absolute necessity of real faith for salvation, he may admit the existence of a person who, as an apparent unbeliever, as an "anonymous" Christian, is presented with the concrete possibility of faith in the real sense of the word. This is true because he is gripped, interiorly moved and prompted by supernatural, elevating grace, and it does not necessarily mean that he has already been reached by official revelation, occurring in history, coming to him in explicit statements.

The *second* premise (accepted by all Thomists) is the modification of consciousness which always accompanies any supernatural "raising" of man's spiritual activity by supernatural, saving, grace. This premise is rejected by those who claim that even when man is seized and prompted by grace, even when grace is present, divinizing him, lifting him up, and exerting real effects on his spiritual activity, he may experience no conscious difference from a man who lacks such grace and whose spiritual activity is purely natural. For them, supernatural grace would remain outside the scope of man's awareness. But the Thomist asserts that such is not the case. This Thomistic conception of the ontological nature of supernatural grace—both in being *and* in awareness—does not maintain that consciousness is modified *in its content,* so that a specific object hitherto totally unknown could dawn upon it. This change in consciousness is to be conceived as wholly unthematic, not affecting any content. This may happen in two quite different ways.

First because an object presented "from without" enters as a single object into the wider reaches of consciousness and is grasped therein *under* this previously given, co-conscious, unthematic horizon of consciousness acting as a selective principle, or a schema of apperception, and so on, as under a formal object given apriori. Thus a pagan may hear something from without in a sermon about the Trinity. He may hear it with or without grace, he may accept or reject what he hears. But his consciousness may as a result be modified thematically and in its contents.

Secondly, a modification of consciousness is theoretically

possible when the apriori formal object, the horizon of consciousness as such, is modified. Suppose, for instance, that
through a divine intervention the eye should be modified in
such a way that it could also see infrared and ultraviolet
"colors" and perceive all light vibrations within this increased
range of sensitivity. Suppose further that in fact only red is
presented to it, as before. Then the eye sees the former red,
it sees no other color (no infrared is object of this particular
act of vision); yet it sees the former red in a different way,
within a wider range of vision. And this new horizon is conscious (co-conscious in the perception of the former red),
although it is not an object of the act of seeing and although
the eye itself cannot reflect upon this new range of perception
and turn the infrared into an object *of sight*. If this new range
of vision (the new apriori formal object) did not emerge into
consciousness, if it were altogether unconscious, the eye could
not, as it were, look out for infrared and wait for it. It would
be unable to see red as "not infrared." The horizon of consciousness of the several cognitive powers is unthematically
known, even when it is not an object of consciousness and
even when reflection on it is perhaps impossible.

In connection with this second premise the Thomist grants
readily and as a matter of course that elevating grace does not
necessarily mean a thematic modification of consciousness
affecting its content. Yet he will firmly maintain that this does
not imply that grace is beyond the reach of consciousness. It
may bring about a modification of consciousness of the second
kind, a change in the unthematic horizon within which the
(religious) realities given from without are apperceived. In
order to understand this, we have only to think of the transcendental implication of being. We remember that the latter

means only this: even when we are engrossed in everyday things, we grasp them always already within the universal horizon of being, although the latter never becomes thematic. Yet should we not know this horizon, we would be unable to know anything; outside the context of this horizon we would be unable to think. Likewise we would be unable to think without knowing logic, yet we might never have heard anything about logical principles. Nevertheless we can think only insofar as we think logically, insofar as logic is simply, as it were, the unthematic, unobjectively known instrument of all our thinking.

So when we speak of this unobjectivated, anonymous, silently presupposed "horizon consciousness," we mean that divine grace, which permeates man's spiritual life, supplies for him not necessarily an object hitherto unknown, but an unthematic "horizon consciousness" *under* which he knows everything else. He may be unable to make this horizon consciousness thematic, to reflect upon it. But it is "there." It is there in utter stillness, as when somebody is soundlessly enveloped by the loving presence of another, of which he need not be thematically aware but which he, nevertheless, clearly experiences. And he may experience it in such a way that it seems to change him entirely. Not only does it seem to change him, it effects a change in his consciousness. If a human being can bring about such an alteration in another, why might not supernatural grace do the same, modifying a man's whole outlook and making him see things in a new light?

Starting from the two premises we have outlined, we may say *in the third place:* this universal bestowal of grace, which through God's salvific will is offered to all men, this actual but entitatively supernatural, divine inner communication which transforms consciousness, may rightfully be considered as a kind of *revelation*. True, this revelation is not immediately as such the communication of objective knowledge expressed in statements, but it must nevertheless be conceived as the communication of some knowledge by a freely acting God, even if this knowledge is unthematic and present only as a horizon. It is something which falls under the concept of revelation properly so called. It is true that this revelation, with its peculiar features, is not what we usually mean by revelation. If Holy Scripture says: God is just, and if God has revealed this statement, in this case "revelation" is the communication of a statement expressed in concepts and emerging in our consciousness as an *object* of knowledge. Revelation may undoubtedly assume this form. But it would be arbitrary to claim that it always does, that it can occur *only* by way of communication of an object, of a statement. Only if we erroneously maintain that knowledge always means objective knowledge, expressed in statements and concepts, can we deny that the unthematic modification of consciousness by way of horizon may also mean a real modification of consciousness. Only then can we state that this kind of intervention cannot constitute the communication of a conscious content to this consciousness, a knowledge freely given by God, hence a self-revelation through self-communication in that grace which ultimately is God himself.

It is erroneous to identify knowing with knowing in statements. This is evident from the fact of subjective implication. Knowledge or awareness should not be identified with express, thematic knowledge, not even when eventually man's spiritual and free consciousness explicitly denies such an unthematic horizon consciousness, represses and suppresses it, refuses to

acknowledge it. This may occur not only through unbelief
—unthematic unbelief—in the case of God's revelation by
inner grace. It may happen also in the case of a natural
horizon consciousness, as, for instance, when a "sensist" asserts
with regard to logic, which he experiences unthematically as
spiritual and universally valid, that it consists only of acci-
dental mechanisms in his brain, which might equally have been
different. But if fundamentally different kinds of knowledge
exist—thematic knowledge and knowledge by way of horizon,
or, according to Heidegger, *Befindlichkeitswissen* (knowledge
by way of an ontological disposition)—then, theoretically,
both forms of knowledge may be communicated by God, so
that supernatural unthematic knowledge by way of horizon is
really "revelation."

Once we have come so far, the statement from which we
started imposes itself: the universal history of salvation is, by
its very definition, the universal history of revelation. Hence
if and insofar as all human beings of all times and all places
stand under the influence of divine, elevating, supernatural
grace, they experience revelation. Not in the sense that God
communicates statements to them and guarantees these as
true, but in the sense that they are endowed with a real
horizon consciousness brought about by divine grace. This
means that the history of revelation is co-extensive with the
history of grace, and vice versa. If we grant, on account of
the universal salvific will, that the history of grace extends to
all times, all peoples and every single individual, we have in
this sense a right to say: the history of revelation extends to
all men, to every individual. However, inasmuch as the revelation given by grace differs from the revelation which takes
place through objective statements, we distinguish a universal

revelation bestowed by grace and a special thematic revelation presented in statements. Hence that which is usually called the history of revelation by the prophets and by Jesus Christ is not simply identical with *the* history of revelation. It is only a particular aspect of it, only revelation in express statements, proclaimed by the prophets or by Jesus Christ in the name of God. It is, as it were, thematic, explicit revelation, which is important because, among other reasons, it is only through statements and words that we come into touch with others. Hence, also, it is only this revelation expressed in statements which is sociological, institutional, corporate.

What, then, is the relation between the universal revelation deriving from grace and occurring everywhere and the revelation which takes place at determined points in time and space —special, thematic, verbalized revelation? We shall understand this relation if we reflect upon the general relation between unthematic horizon consciousness and verbalized, conceptual thematic knowledge; thus, for instance, on the relation between man's unthematic logical knowledge and his explicit, theoretical, official logic. We have already said that a person who has never heard of logic experiences himself as logical in the basic structure of his mind, and that ultimately we understand logic as a science, or as a set of logical rules understood in a rather primitive way (after all, everybody is not a scientist), only if we possess this fundamental disposition. On the other hand, we must also say that this disposition strives towards verbalization, towards the reflexive accessibility of explicit logic. The two aspects condition each other. The reflexive aspect presupposes the non-reflexive aspect. The latter, by its very nature, tries to objectivate itself in a reflexive expression; horizon consciousness tends towards objectivation.

Whether this basic arrangement is a natural one—as, for instance, the basic structure "time"—or a supernatural one, we can react correctly to it only if we reflect on it in concepts and statements, at least to some extent—an extent which may differ *very* much from person to person and may be at times reduced to almost nothing. Whatever we know objectively, in verbalized knowledge, presupposes some unthematic awareness. The relation between these two elements may vary considerably. On the other hand, the whole basic structure strives by its very nature towards this thematic translation in express terms.

If we apply all this to the problem of the relation between universal historical revelation carried by grace on the one hand, and the verbalized, particular, special history of salvation on the other hand, we may say: the special history of salvation is nothing but the thematization of the universal history of revelation, as directed by God and guaranteed in its truth by miracles. Throughout the universal history of salvation there is the communication of grace as the grace of Christ; from the beginning the whole process points towards the Incarnation, and always, already is based upon it.

If we look at it now from the other side, we see that the universal history of revelation is nothing but the universal history of salvation, becoming thematic in the special history of revelation. For in the special history of salvation, as it developed from Moses through the Prophets to Jesus Christ, man is told in explicit statements what God has wrought for him in the history of salvation; hence what has really occurred. The history of salvation is really history in which something happens. And in this history, in every event something is also "revealed." Since in the universal history of salvation the event is grace —that is, not merely an objective occurrence but something which by its very nature involves consciousness of it—we can say in a real sense that with every event something is also revealed in the sphere of an unthematic, subjectively implicit, transcendental consciousness. And it is only on this as a foundation that the public history of revelation unfolds, as the divinely directed reflection on, and the historical manifestation and explicitation of, this supernatural universal history of revelation and salvation. This history of salvation itself, as such—that is, as a communication of grace—has its own history. This is evident from the fact that although grace is continually given, from the beginning the process is directed towards the Incarnation and the hypostatic union as the absolute union of God (grace) and the world, because the self-communication of God becomes complete and irrevocable only in this event. In this sense the transcendental history of salvation, and not only its categorical explicitation in words—that is, the public, special history of revelation—is real history. Hence the universal history *and* the special public history of salvation and revelation meet in Jesus Christ and reach their fulfillment in him in the fullness of time. Grace working in the universal history of salvation and revelation reaches the fullness of its external manifestation in Christ's revelation of himself, and hence, fundamentally, the history of special revelation is offered to all men as widely and universally as the universal history of salvation and revelation.

In the history of the developing reflection on the universal history of salvation we must once more distinguish the reflection done by man (although it is, as it were, set in motion by God and to some extent directed by him) and the reflection officially guaranteed by God. Let us take the case of a Neanderthal man, who lived about 100,000 years before Christ. We must admit of him that in the depths of his being he was aware of some reality like "God," even though he was unable to say much about his *Grundbefindlichkeit,* this theism which he experienced but hardly reflected on. Yet this theism may have been a theism deriving from supernatural elevation, the supernatural proximity of God, the supernatural mercy of God. Let us suppose that this Neanderthal man starts, unavoidably, to reflect upon this spiritual, supernatural "basic disposition" —whatever may have been the "literary genre" of these reflections, however mythlike it may have been. This sets in motion a theological process of reflection on universal revelation, be the scale ever so humble. Whether Neanderthal man or some other human being reflects in this way, such a reflection upon the content of the universal history of revelation through grace may "succeed" or fail: it can be ingenious or very primitive, use very sublime concepts or express itself more in the plastic form of myths or of the dance, or in some other way. Whatever the way or the medium in which it expresses itself, this reflection is always—not only but also— a reflection upon the "transcendental" experience of the universal supernatural history of salvation.

Whether we should call such a reflection on this universal supernatural revelation "special" revelation—insofar as God is, as it were, interested in it and favors it—is rather a question of terminology. It is customary to speak of "special" revelation only when such a verbalized thematization of the universal history of revelation, as practiced by man in every religion, is guaranteed in its truth by God. In this case the "prophet," the bearer of revelation, is the man who, "moved" by God's grace and given divine auspices through his marvelous self-manifestation, message and deeds, proclaims in statements what has already been known to some extent in an unthematic, unconceptualized way through universal revelation. All this the prophet now communicates to the multitudes in a prophetic authoritative way, under divine guarantee. "Thus speaks Yahweh."

Of course, the universal history of salvation and of revelation is translated by the prophet under divine guarantee not only in a *general* "categorical" way, but also in the context of a special situation of salvation or of doom in his own people and his own history. Thus this situation is explained in an unequivocal and authoritative manner in its positive or negative relation to the basic happening of the universal history of salvation and revelation. And this explanation ("covenant," "breaking of the covenant") carries the divine warrant, as well as the general categorical translation of universal revelation into special revelation. Nor should we overlook the fact that this explanation is a moment in the history of salvation itself.

What do these considerations mean for our problem of the necessity of faith for salvation, for the problem from which we started? This problem was: How is it possible that *every* human being, wherever or whenever he may live, enjoys the possibility of performing an act of faith, since such an act must be a Yes to a divine revelation in the proper sense? Not every human being seems to be reached by such a revelation, not even by the revelation which may have occurred in Paradise.

We answer as follows: Since, according to the principles of theology, we must not only admit a special revelation, but we may, without clashing with these principles, at least hope for a universal revelation given in and with grace, it may be stated that everyone has a possibility of saying Yes to this *universal* revelation which reaches *every human being,* while not everyone is reached by "special" revelation.

We say this not with the intention of convincing the unbeliever that he *says* such a Yes. But the *believer* should be convinced that the unbeliever says it. He should understand that this Yes is spoken by the so-called unbeliever and can be spoken by him. For it is truly not correct to argue as follows: Man can find his salvation only through faith. But this faith presupposes a real revelation of God. Now such a revelation is to be found only in the special history of revelation, and therefore any attempt to discover the possibility of an act of faith outside the special history of salvation will from the start lead nowhere. This line of argument is false. For theology itself declares that there is a history of revelation which is universally accessible to all, insofar as it is but the communication of divine grace to every human being. Theology further states that, on account of the universal and seriously intended salvific will of God we must, or at least we may, accept that such a grace is available to every man. Hence with the universal history of revelation every man receives the possibility of realizing the faith required for salvation. So the only problem which remains is to find out how the faith looks which is based only upon the universal supernatural history of salvation and revelation and not upon the special verbalized form of it. How does this faith work? What content does it acquire, even though only unthematically? What content must it acquire in order to be a really salvific faith?

For an answer to these questions we turn again to theology. It is theologically correct to say that faith is salvific when it is a belief in God as the author of the moral order. At least this theory is not condemned by the magisterium; it is satisfied with a content which does not differ materially from a purely natural knowledge of God. Should one object that a natural metaphysical knowledge is not faith, we would first reply that every religious truth remains a religious truth even when it can be known naturally. Next we would say that this knowledge has never been developed by the individual person left to his own devices. Even the philosopher who thinks in a purely abstract way will not claim that his metaphysical constructions come wholly from his own mind unaided. There are always statements he has learned from hearing, which are ready to hand, borrowed from a tradition. The thinker who borrows them treats them with respect, even when he assimilates the transmitted truth through personal insight. He respects them because, at least in the domain of religious truth, the concrete person, even when autonomously rethinking tradition, does not emancipate himself from this truth but assimilates it in a real way. Finally, every man is situated in the supernatural order, he is situated and lives in it in such a way that he is sustained and grasped by grace. If it is true that he is situated within the horizon of supernatural universal revelation, although the latter may be unthematic, then his—more or less explicit—metaphysical affirmation of God is necessarily more than a mere metaphysical affirmation, even though this added dimension does not become thematic. The horizon of the statement imparts to it implicitly another character (in accordance with this horizon and its range) than it would have if man studied this metaphysics "in the state of pure nature." Thus this horizon makes natural metaphysical knowledge supernatural, and that which, so far as its content is concerned, seems to be no more than "rational truth" and mere metaphysics, acquires in a subjectively implicit way the quality of being God's voice, a testimony from a higher power. This is true even if such knowledge makes no express distinction between natural knowledge and knowledge produced by grace, and if the act of knowledge is not reflexively known as an act of faith.

6 / The Specific Christian Content of This Faith

Towards the end of the last chapter we said that there is a theological theory, not condemned by the magisterium, which holds that for faith to be salvific it is sufficient for it to contain a belief in the existence of God as the guarantor of the moral order. This position is quite encouraging for our inquiry into the possibility of salvation for the "anonymous Christian." Yet, from the point we have now reached, we must demonstrate the possibility that in the act of faith performed by the "anonymous Christian" on the basis of universal revelation more is actually contained in subjective implication than this materially considered, abstract theism. The anonymous Christian is also much more Christian in the content of his faith than most theologians seem to admit and venture to demand.

But first a little more about subjective implication, so that the thesis we wish to establish may not seem simpler and more obvious than it is.

Let us suppose that somebody should profess absolute materialism with the statement "Truth is that which is useful for man." Yet the same materialist might be unable to tell an untruth, even when this inability results in considerable

damage to himself. Should we not say in such a case that
basically it does not matter how the person in question stands
explicitly with regard to truth; that it does not matter whether
truth exists for him explicitly; whether explicitly he does not
believe in truth, since his way of *living up* to truth is evidently
not hampered thereby? Likewise the fact that somebody "believes" explicitly does not mean much if he implicitly lives a
life of unbelief. "Subjective implication"[1] means that the
"implicit" is thought and known, in a real if peculiar way—
that it has real effects on a man. For what purpose would be
served by co-contained statements if they were only objectively
implicit so far as their content is concerned? Only that which
reaches a man can help him see the truth. Only then can he
live up to it; live up to a real faith grounded in this truth; live
up to this faith, which, if it is to be Christian faith, should
mean: the Trinity, the Incarnation, supernatural grace. Should
the specific Christian content of the faith, falling under the universal history of grace and revelation, be involved only in an
objectively implicit way in man's "acceptance of existence,"
the anonymous Christian would have neither more nor less
concern with it than the non-mathematician with higher mathematics. The latter, too, are contained in germ in first-grade
arithmetic, as the truths of the Trinity, the Incarnation and
grace are contained in man's supernatural faith in God as the
guarantor of the moral order.

Of such a faith theology declares, without challenge, that it

[1] Should we be accused of repeating things which have been said
often enough, we shall answer: they cannot be said often enough! For
one still continually meets explanations of "explicit" and "implicit"
which do not do justice to the real meaning of these ideas, especially
where "implicit" should be understood as *subjectively* implicit, and yet
is not.

has a content which, although minimal, is yet sufficient for salvation. As against this moderation and broadmindedness, we might wonder whether, despite Hebr. 11:6, such a content really is enough to make faith salvific. The answer might be that this content "objectively" implies all that is specifically Christian. But is that enough? For faith is necessary for salvation not in the sense of a moral prerequisite, but as the beginning of the possession of salvation itself. But can salvation be reached when the content of faith is possessed only "objectively"; when, subjectively, there is a total failure to reach or possess it? Is it, then, necessary to be so modest in our demands as theology here feels *allowed* to be because it feels *obliged* to be so broadminded if it is unwilling to deny the possibility of salvation to many people? If such moderation is not to be necessary, we should have to show that all the Christian elements required to make faith fully and specifically a Christian faith leading to salvation are also actually present in the anonymous Christian, although only by way of *subjective* implication.

Almost everybody sooner or later experiences the peculiar difficulty presented by the sheer complexity of Christian dogmatic development—an unexpected complexity, indeed, in a religion which claims to be *the* religion required for salvation for *all* men. It is as if God were unable to get across to the average human being what he must know in order to reach salvation; as if a whole system of theories and ratiocinations were necessary. When what is at stake is salvation—that is, the bare survival of the individual, average man who must work out his salvation in a struggle with the harsh and insecure conditions of daily life—religion seems to stand in need of a simple system which everybody can manage, of a short, easy-to-learn formula, one that can in fact be known and practiced by everybody, and not only by those who make it their business to dispute about the various ways of explaining their theories.

We should not underestimate the difficulty which this fact presents for modern man. His impression is not that Christian doctrine has too little content. On the contrary, he feels that Christian knowledge has exceeded all bounds, and that it is arrogant when it makes its appeal to God for all that is known. When, because of the complexity of its statements and their ramifications, theology gets lost in difficulties which could have been avoided from the start by a greater simplicity in the system, it hastens to appeal to "faith." When there is absolutely no further way out, then its last recourse is an appeal to "the mystery."

What we say here indicates whither we are heading. We wish to show that there is indeed a simple "formula," manageable by everybody, to which Christianity can be reduced, and that precisely when the Christian faith seems to become enmeshed in difficulties and takes refuge in "the mystery," its meaning is basically something very simple.

This does not remove the possibility that this simple content may be stated and explained in the most complex and sublime way. We wish to show that man, the anonymous Christian included, can in fact know all he must know for salvation in an implicit manner—that is, as something apprehended in subjective implication. In *subjective,* not merely in objective, implication. Hence not in the way one would know, for instance, the concrete data involved in the botanical system of Linnaeus. He who knows something about such a system in general does not co-know these facts; he can know them only if somebody teaches them to him from without.

We do not mean that the latter kind of knowledge plays no part in the Christian knowledge of faith, a knowledge which has reference to objects that can be known either in an objectively *im*plicit way only, or in a subjectively *ex*plicit manner only through an express verbalized communication from without. In the case of Christian dogmatic statements about concrete historical events in man's world of experience, knowledge is possible only by way of merely objective implication. Either one hears of them from without and knows them in a merely empirical way, or when positive experience or information from without is lacking, one does not know them.

Moreover, we do not claim that the knowledge of such concrete statements does not matter for man's religion. Since ultimately they are statements of the faith, it is concerned with them. They share the mysterious character of the faith because they belong to the totality of the mysteries of salvation in the strict sense. Since this faith is a faith unto salvation, such contingent historical statements are important for salvation. But it is the object itself which matters, which influences the life and salvation of man. It is not necessary that he should have a detailed and express knowledge of it. Thus he may live without knowing anything about the chemistry of digestion, although it is an important factor in biological life and underlies the process of metabolism. Likewise he may believe and live up to his faith in a Christian way without knowing all the data belonging to the content of this faith. It is often impossible, even in relatively ideal cases, to know all these data specifically, because often they belong to historical and social contexts which cannot be known, or not known with precision, by many people. Such are, for instance, the place and date of Christ's birth, the concrete manner of his death, the name of the woman who was his mother, the fact that he established a community of those who believe in him and that he chose one out of this group to be his vicar on earth. All these facts are part of the data of the faith, they are important for salvation, taught authoritatively or even defined by the Church; yet not every human being need know them as part of his subjective knowledge. We should not forget that man is of his very nature such that he can precisely *not* know and embrace all that is important for his existence.

Hence we should not claim either that a "contingent historical truth" cannot be important for our existence or that all that is religiously important must also be really known. It is not with knowledge alone—not even with subjectively implicit knowledge—that man must face the unforeseeable, contingent and utterly fortuitous events of his life, even when they matter for his destiny. There *must* be for him an element of the unforeseen which he accepts in an altogether "blind" way, which he cannot discover even through subjectively implicit knowledge. For it belongs to human nature to be "blind" like one who steps onto a bridge not knowing whether it will bear his weight. In this way the concrete historical facts of Christianity, all that is merely aposteriori, need not be known and, as it were, possessed by man in the way he knows and possesses in subjective implication—hence not "blindly"—what he is told in the general history of revelation by God himself; the formula for which we have been searching, which summarizes the whole content of Christianity: that God has given himself to man in immediate proximity.

For this formula, and for it alone, we demand the possibility of a subjective implication, because in it we have the basic conception of God as a God who is near to us, because all specifically Christian truths may be reduced to it, because in this formula we have the mystery, the basic mystery, to which all mysteries of faith can be reduced. We speak of a revelation which, as general revelation, reaches, or at least *can* reach, all men; this general revelation consists in the communication of grace itself; in virtue of the universal salvific will we may—nay, we must—expect that this grace will reach every man. It follows that in this grace every man is enabled to acknowledge the basic mystery and, with it, the faith which is specifically Christian, even when the so-called special, public revelation has not come his way.

Two questions arise in this connection: First, why and how can the basic mystery be admitted in this faith? Secondly, why and how does "the mystery" implicitly contain all that specifically Christian faith contains—how can the complexity of Christian dogma be contained in such a simple statement —so that one who knows "the mystery" knows in a subjectively implicit way all that he must know by way of specific Christian faith if he wishes to be saved?

We have said above what Christian theology means by a "mystery." A distinction is made between the absolute mystery and that which, although mysterious, is not the absolute mystery, not *mysterium stricte dictum*. As Christian *mysteria stricte dicta* we have mentioned the following three: Trinity, Incarnation and supernatural grace. Now we claim that the mystery, the simple "formula," is the last, all-embracing mystery, the basic mystery, in which the three affirmations of the Trinity, the Incarnation and grace are implicitly co-contained.

They are co-contained because the two last affirmations mean
a *self*-communication of God to man, because the first affirmation refers to the Trinity as the necessary foundation of this
double self-communication of God, and because "the mystery"
means precisely: God has given himself to man in *absolute*
nearness.

What is meant by the *self*-communication of God? First it
does not mean the communication of something distinct from
God, which would not be God himself, which could express
something *about* him only in an indirect way. In such a communication God would indeed freely communicate *himself,*
insofar as all that God produces says something about him
as its creator. Thus creation undoubtedly is a revelation of
God, but only in the sense that God makes himself known in
it as the creator of this new reality; in this sense the world
gives testimony to God and points to him. To this extent it is
a natural gift and revelation of God, but one in which man is
still limited to the order of nature and of analogy. In this kind
of natural revelation God is always "mediated"—represented
by something distinct from himself, by something which brings
him to us only as the remote one, the one who keeps his
distance, the one who does not really give himself, but only
gives creatures which are not he. In the supernatural order it
is the giver himself who becomes the gift. So here we speak
of self-communication because the Infinite himself is given to
the finite. God gives himself in his own innermost reality, so
that the ultimate reality in man and about man, where his
destiny and the fulfillment of his existence are concerned, must
be called God himself. Not, of course, as if man should become God. He remains always the one who is not God. For
it is not his own essence which he attains in this divine reality.

When he experiences it as the innermost reality of his own existence, which "comes to itself" only by reaching the "super essential" in person, this comes as a thing *received* and not as that without which he cannot realize his own essence and nature.

This experience of the divine, of the absolute, presents a problem which one meets time and again in the general history of religion, as when the question arises how we should interpret this experience of the absolute. Is it an experience of an ultimate, absolute and divine element in man himself, so that man may say that in his innermost being he experiences *himself*, his most personal "I"? Not, of course, the individual, bodily, contingent "I", but that ultimate, spiritual I, which remains, as it were, when all that which is only terrestrial and inessential has been transcended and left behind, so that in such an experience it is possible to say that man comes wholly to himself.

From the Christian point of view and in the light of the Christian interpretation of experience, this interpretation carries no great weight. Still, Christian faith too speaks of the experience of an *absolute* self-communication of God in which God himself becomes the innermost reality of the created spirit. With this in mind we might be able to understand how, when the human spirit reaches self-awareness in the ground of its being, man might think: this is myself, I am God. But, as we have said, this interpretation carries no great weight, it is false and contradicts all religious experience. In Christianity we find precisely the true and adequate interpretation of this primordial experience of the absolute nearness of the mystery. In this "ecstasy," in this total and most sublime union between man and God, on this pinnacle, man experiences himself as the being who falls on his knees in adoration. So when Christianity speaks of the self-communication of God to man, it means the marvel of freely proffered love, not due to human nature, on which—and this makes it a marvel—man has no claim by virtue of his nature, and especially not as the sinner he is. He receives it as grace, and, since it is not due to his nature, as a supernatural grace.

We have already spoken of the two ways in which this self-communication of God occurs—the Incarnation and grace—and of the truth on which they are founded and presuppose —the Trinity. These three realities, the basic truths of Christianity, are co-contained for man implicitly—by way of subjective implication—in the fundamental mystery of God's absolute nearness to him.

Let us first consider the mystery of grace. It should be easy to understand that, when man experiences the nearness of the "mystery" as it shelters him and accepts him in pardoning and forbearing love, when he welcomes this experience, he thereby implicitly accepts supernatural grace. He accepts it insofar as the absolute nearness of God to man means the absolute self-communication of God to man in all the dimensions of man's spiritual existence, so that God is not only the distant, asymptotic goal of all his strivings but the one he really reaches, not through his own powers but because God has drawn utterly close to him in a spontaneous movement. But this is precisely what Christianity teaches about supernatural grace. It presents "grace"—sanctifying, justifying grace—as the divine nature itself, the beatifying content of man's future life, already here on earth offered to the believer. Not that it is possible simply to deduce the doctrine of supernatural grace from the statement that man has the absolute experience of

God's nearness, sheltering and welcoming him. For a certain ambiguity is attached to man's experience of this proximity by its very nature, and when he reflects upon it conceptually he may have lingering doubts that it is a real experience of the radical, unsurpassed self-communication of God's innermost splendor. But we discover in this experience of God's absolute nearness at least sufficient convergence with the doctrine of grace to allow the Christian positively to say that the non-Christian also experiences divine grace in the experience of the sheltering and loving nearness of the absolute mystery called God. When he accepts this mystery as the mystery of forgiving love, he accepts supernatural grace in faith, with a belief founded in real subjective implication.

It is more difficult, however, to make clear why such a trustful, welcoming acceptance in faith of the experience of the absolute nearness of the mystery implies the acceptance of the mystery of the Incarnation as well. We recur first to a point made several times before: a free acceptance of the mystery that is beyond our control, which holds sway over us, always means a courageous yielding to the unforeseeable, the unfathomable. It means a yielding to, a trusting in, a movement whose hidden term is truly accepted in a subjectively implicit way through this act of total confidence. When man allows the unfathomable to dispose of him, to draw closer to him, and welcomes its approach, he is never able to foresee the degree of nearness intended and to be attained by this approach. And thus he does not know what intensity it will reach, how unreservedly the God who offers himself in utmost intimacy will give himself to the man who welcomes him. Yet in this way he accepts the full *potentialities* of such a movement from God's side; he accepts its direction, and thereby

also (although not expressly) that extreme point towards
which such an advancing divine self-communication, freely
accepted and freely accomplished, is moving and can move.
One who accepts the love of another person undergoes a
similar experience: he knows, yet does not know, whither
such an acceptance leads, so that the destiny and the history
of such a love are at once unexpected and obvious. They are
obvious because in the term of this love whose development
could not be anticipated, the lover finds precisely what he had
really accepted and in a certain sense foreseen from the
start. The same thing happens when man accepts the love of
God drawing him into intimacy: "knowing" the unfathomable,
he also already accepts the uttermost possibilities of this love.

If we wish to comprehend how the acceptance of God as
the mystery of absolute proximity subjectively implies the
acceptance of the Incarnation we must, in the second place,
consider the following: the Incarnation may, or rather must,
be conceived as the unparalleled instance of the proximity of
God to man. First as a divine proximity to the humanity of
Jesus which makes of Christ a human being not less, but more,
than we are, although, or rather because, he is not a human
person. Next, and as a consequence, as such a drawing near
to all men. The nature of man should be seen as the openness
—as the opening up—of a spirit to the absolute mystery, as
the self-donation of the creature to God—such a self-donation
as anticipates its acceptance by God, or entertains this as a
possibility, because God offers himself to man. Thus the self-
donation of man is experienced from the start as a response
to a divine self-offering to the finite spiritual creature, and
the Incarnation must be seen as the supreme, the unique, unparalleled instance of this relationship, in which the response

of the creature itself is sustained by the self-offering of God; and at the same time the response by which the creature gives itself to God reaches its goal, as it were, in an absolute way, as the highest instance, unmatched by any other, of what belongs to man's nature, especially to man's nature as raised supernaturally by grace.[2]

Of course, when the person who ventures into the relation of total nearness with God has a glimpse of the pinnacle of its intensity, he does not yet know concretely in whom this supreme ideal of such a proximity has been reached. He cannot, in the context of his experience, put a historical name to this realization. But he has ventured into a movement which brings God and man nearer to each other, and he experiences this movement as one of absolute love, as a movement which strives towards ever increasing closeness. Already he dimly foresees that somewhere, at some time, a point must be reached at which God, who communicates himself, and the man who accepts this communication become united in the strictest ontological and personal sense.

In the third place, as concerns the mystery of the Trinity, we must now try to "derive" it, as it were, from the special characteristic of the divine self-communication, so as to understand how this mystery too is contained in what we call the basic mystery: the absolute nearness of God to man. Here we must keep the following point in mind: in this special characteristic of the divine self-communication to man whereby the

---

[2] Cp. for these considerations, which cannot be further developed here: B. Welte, *Homoousios hemin*, in *Das Konzil von Chalkedon*, Vol. III, Wurzburg, 1951; and K. Rahner, *Schriften zur Theologie*, Einsiedeln, 3, 1958, and IV, 1961. In English: K. Rahner, *Spiritual Exercises*, New York, 1965, pp. 97 ff.

"Father" communicates himself through the "Son" in the "Holy Spirit" (so that God communicates himself as the "triune" God), this "threeness" in the divine self-communication, the "Trinity of the economy of Salvation" (*heilsokonomische Dreifaltigkeit*), does not refer only to three aspects which the one God assumes only because, and insofar as, he is communicating himself to man. For then the trinity would be no more than the "outward modality" of such an activity. If the "trinity" were *only* a datum of the economy of salvation, this would not enable us to discover how God proceeds in his own inner reality. We would not be able to see that the life within the Godhead, too, has the nature of donation, of a self-communication of the Father to the Son and of the Father and the Son to the Holy Spirit. In that event we would not understand how Christian faith, which is a belief in God as the triune God, is implicitly contained in the basic mystery of the absolute nearness of God, or, more precisely, in its realization through the Incarnation and supernatural grace. In that case, "the Trinity of the economy of salvation" would be only the manner in which God wrought man's salvation, it would exist only in man's mind, not in God himself. Trinity would not be something which belongs to God in and for himself, independently of any such outside activity, of any creation and communication in grace to this creation. Trinity would only be the way man experiences salvation, not the experience of that which God is in his most intimate being. In that case we could not say that there is a real self-communication of God. He would not be "in himself" what he is "for us," he would not have given himself in his innermost reality. It follows that the Trinity of the "economy of salvation" must be the "immanent" Trinity—that is, the difference in the process of divine self-communication (Father-Son-Holy Spirit) must belong to God in himself, as he is independently of his free self-communication to us.

It is not our intention to deduce a complete doctrine of the Trinity from this subjective experience of revelation. Within the history of revelation this doctrine has developed only gradually. It states that the divine nature is communicated by the Father to the Son through a process of pure spiritual generation, by the uttering of the Word; likewise the Holy Spirit receives the divine nature from the Father and the Son through an act of love, while the "Father" himself is the unoriginated source of Son and Holy Spirit. About this self-communication within the Godhead, insofar as it is essential for the life of God within himself, theology teaches that, when God communicates himself outside himself, the latter *self-communication* is like the one which takes place eternally in God himself. The distinction between "Father," "Son" and "Holy Spirit" is not only a differentiation which takes place in the relation between God and creature in this divine self-communication but is that which defines God in himself.

When we mention this doctrine, we do not mean to say that we can, out of this subjective experience of revelation alone and with unaided human reason, demonstrate the Christian doctrine of the Trinity to individual men. But one point seems to follow from what we have said: it is quite conceivable that in this experience of the absolute proximity of God in Christ and in grace, the mystery of the Trinity too is grasped in subjective implication, even though this experience, as that of an individual, cannot yet objectivate itself in a complete, explicit doctrine of the Trinity. The Trinity, the Incarnation and supernatural grace cannot, in their express meaning, be discovered in a purely autonomous process of explicitation. What would be the function of public, special historical revelation if this were possible? It would be as superfluous as a public, historical revelation whereby God told man that he is a logical being. Man knows this of himself, for he can by his own powers develop the subjectively implicit logic of his spiritual existence in an objectified scientific logic. If he could do the same thing with subjectively implicit Christianity, this would mean that, having grace, he would need only to look into himself with sufficient attention to discover within himself the whole catechism. Such an explanation of the origin of the official, conceptual doctrine of the faith would still not be "modernism," or a theology or apologetics of immanence in the modernist sense. For its "immanent" starting point would be freely granted, supernatural grace—that is, in the last analysis, the personal God who enters into dialog with man. Yet it would present a too "immanentistic" explanation of the public and special history of revelation, conceiving it as an almost "natural" process rooted solely in the nature of man as a being who reflects.

But all this is far removed from our own considerations. They do not deduce explicit Christianity from anonymous Christianity; they show explicit Christianity that it follows from its own data, which are explicitly known only to itself, that there must be some such thing as anonymous Christianity, and that the essence of Christianity may be contained in it in a subjective manner which cannot be autonomously explicitated. Thus the non-Christian may be made to understand that he is not as far removed from official Christianity as he may think himself. And the professed Christian may realize to what a very simple and at the same time infinite mystery the multiplicity of his theological formulas may be reduced.

Our purpose is simply to show the convergence between that which the anonymous Christian and every human being, as interiorly elevated by grace, experiences, or can experience, and that which public, historical Christianity teaches explicitly.

7/ Anonymous Christianity as a Religious and Moral Task

Every human being is a Christian, and he is one not always expressly but very often anonymously. This statement, which summarizes what we have said up to now, raises the question of the relation between anonymous Christianity and man's moral decision about this Christianity of his. When we assert that everybody is a Christian at least anonymously, we shall rightly be asked why any need should remain for a free moral decision in favor of the faith. Why do we require from the explicit Christian an act of faith, a personal free decision to believe? Why do we ask more from him than from the anonymous Christian, since there is an anonymous Christianity, since everybody is a Christian, explicitly or implicitly? If all human beings are Christians—explicitly or implicitly— why should faith still be required as a moral decision of man necessary for salvation?

All men are Christians in some way, although the ways differ very widely. That is a fact. But this fact does not answer the question whether a man's eternal destiny will be salvation or doom. It only gives him the possibility of making it into salvation. It will become salvation if he accepts his Christi-

anity in a free moral decision. It will turn into doom if, with
the same freedom, he rejects his Christianity. Acceptance or
rejection—such is the alternative which confronts man, within
which he confronts a Christianity which is, in any event, always given to him. The only question is: does man accept it
by saying the Yes of faith—explicitly or implicitly—or does
he—explicitly or implicitly—say No to it? He may decide in
one way or another, but the decision itself is unavoidable. He
must assume a position in the presence of what he finds, as it
were, from the start as his "given nature," which exists in a
"historical" situation—that is, a situation freely imposed by
God. He must assume an attitude towards everything contained in this nature, all that constitutes it. He cannot think or
act or make a decision without assuming such a position, without saying Yes or No to his being. He may acquiesce in his
finiteness, his poverty, and in the fact that he is doomed to die;
he may also hold out in an attitude of protest against what he
is; he may turn this protest into the innermost feature of his
whole existence, in every utterance, in the everyday details of
this existence. Someone is a woman, and does not want to be a
woman. Her whole life is one act of protest against this fact
that she is a woman. Someone belongs to a certain race and
refuses to accept it. He is a German, and he rejects being a
German. He refuses his whole existence with all its biological
dependence, yet he always remains dependent; no protest of
his takes away what he is by his very nature. Neither can man
abolish this nature through his protest. The special characteristic of the spiritual-personal behavior of this person consists
precisely in the fact that he is what he does not want to be
and that he does not want to be what he is. Ultimately, the

meaning of existence is acquiescence in or refusal of what
one knows oneself to be. Acquiescence and refusal, acceptance
and protest, both aiming at one's nature as the *previous datum*
of one's freedom, both referring to that unavoidable, unremovable dimension of existence within which man first discovers himself, out of which he is, as it were, asked whether
he wishes to say Yes or No to it.

Anonymous Christianity, too, is such an unremovable, unavoidable, absolutely permanent dimension of existence.
Through it man is by historical destination the being whom
God has called to the supernatural vision, whom he has
provided with the offer of his divine intimacy, proximity and
self-communication. Whether he accepts it or not, by his very
nature man is the creature who lives in the purview of the
"mystery," from whom it is asked whether he will trust this
mystery or run away from it, whether he will endeavor to
resist this existential situation which is unalterably imposed
upon him, to forget and to repress it. Hence to the concrete
actual nature of man in the factually existing divine order
belongs not only the abstract essence of man as a spiritual
person, but also his anonymous Christianity. And just as he
may adopt an attitude of refusal with reference to his human
nature in the abstract, or his own sex, his own race, or his age,
likewise with regard to this anonymous Christianity. In this
refusal he shows once more that he has this Christianity, just
as one who rebels at being his age, who wants to be younger
or older, discloses once more that he is precisely what he does
not want to be. It is possible to say that the rejection of such
transcendental necessities of one's nature is done in connection with, or by virtue of, the thing that is rejected.

One who rejects logic[1] rejects it by the power of logic. One who declares that logic is only the cerebral physiological mechanism of human thinking, devoid of any validity, and who presents this interpretation by dint of great dialectical acumen, can do so only by using the power whose existence he denies. Likewise when somebody states that nothing makes sense for him, everything is nonsense, there is no "light," only darkness, insanity, vulgarity. Precisely those who are most opposed to meaning and the light betray thereby that they are filled with the greatest, loftiest and most radical desire for meaning. They would be unable to have such a desire if they did not have an idea of light, of meaning. It would not be possible, if absolute darkness devoid of light were one's natural condition, to wish for light, to protest against the absence of light or to find existence "absurd"; for in order to experience the absence of light, as of meaning, one must be acquainted with light and meaning; only thus is one able to become aware of darkness and absurdity at all. Exactly as it is only one who is not really very stupid who becomes aware of his own stupidity and shows that he is not so stupid by taking this view of himself.

The same thing holds true for the anonymous Christian, whose Christianity exists only by way of refusal, in the form of the No he says to each and every aspect of his existence. Also for that anonymous Christian who, living in the most brutal and absolute loneliness, not only experiences such loneliness and lack of shelter as a misfortune and a form of suffering, but declares with utmost conviction that they constitute the true content of his existence; who freely, consciously

---

[1] The reader is asked to excuse us for using this example of logic so frequently, but it has the great advantage of being "intuitively clear."

and in hatred takes his stand on the insistence that absurdity is all that there is, and in this very insistence betrays the fact that he is one who has some knowledge and experience of not being lonely, of being sheltered, some sense of an element of mystery in his life which is worthy of trust. Let it be added that such a rejection, such a self-identification with the absurd out of a combination of pride and anxiety, need not necessarily take the form of an explicit existential nihilism; it may occur in the average, everyday shape of what the Christian calls "mortal sin," provided, however, that subjective guilt really is involved.

Although this anonymous Christianity is always there, whether one accepts it in inner acquiescence or not, it is not easy to say in concrete individual instances, about either oneself or others, whether it exists by way of acceptance or of refusal, and it can never be said with absolute certainty. Let us come back once more to the example of logic: the one with the most logical mind can argue most convincingly against its existence, before others and for himself; that is, he can act contrary to logic; whereas perhaps the person with a less logical mind may argue in behalf of logic. Thus plenty of logic may be concealed in arguments against it and there may be precious little in arguments on its behalf. (We do not consider here what bearing this has on existential acceptance or rejection.) So likewise the outer image of anonymous Christianity may be very ambiguous. Our judgment is made even more difficult by the fact that there may be implicit acceptance under cover of explicit refusal. The opposite, of course, is also true: under explicit acceptance an implicit rejection may be concealed. Speaking in a quite formal sense, we might distinguish the implicit, subjective datum and its objectively correct or false explicit interpretation; the spiritual, personal, free acceptance of the explicit or of that which is implicitly proffered, and the free personal rejection of the explicit or of the implicit. If we start from this obvious hypothesis (for everything in man, whether explicit or implicit, exists in the manner of free acceptance or free rejection), we have a series of possible modes of existence for man.

The *first* possibility: A person is implicitly a Christian. God has given him this subjectively implicit Christianity by virtue of his universal salvific will. Moreover, this Christianity is freely accepted, first in the dimension of the implicit, but not merely in that dimension. Explicitly too, the person in question knows about Christianity and accepts it. This would be the case of what we may call the "fully developed" Christian, who knows explicitly of his Christianity and accepts this express explicit knowledge in a reflexive free act of faith. That which is given in an express verbalized way and accepted in express reflexive freedom also exists inwardly and implicitly; as a Christianity which is originally proffered to his freedom by anonymous grace and as the implicitly, freely accepted Christianity of the basic acquiescence in existence.

A *second* possibility: The implicit Christianity of hidden grace is proffered and is accepted by the person as anonymous Christianity in his innermost, unreflexive freedom through his acquiescence in existence. He has also heard explicitly of this Christianity but feels, in the domain of verbalized reflection, that he cannot accept it. Thus what he knows conceptually, expressly, of the official doctrine of the Church about the Trinity, he considers as something so contradictory, so absurd, that he rejects it in good faith. Thus he knows of a proffered implicit Christianity *and* of an explicit Christianity. He accepts

the proffered Christianity implicitly in the acceptance of his
own existence. But on the level of the explicit, reflexive,
verbalized conceptualization of this Christianity, he rejects
it. This might well be, nowadays, the situation of many people.
If what we have said about anonymous Christianity is correct, there are people who are permeated within by divine
grace, by the self-communication of God in grace, by the all-
penetrating nearness of the Mystery; and we may definitely
entertain for these men the hope that, whenever they accept
their existence in patience, resignation, in a certain matter-of-
fact way, they also thereby accept the anonymous Christianity
given to them in the depths of their being. This is true even if,
on the level of the explicit, they do not accept the explicitly
proffered Christianity of Catholic or Protestant preaching,
even if explicitly, insofar as their free decision is concerned,
they are not and do not wish to be Christians. But in the
depths of their being there is proffered to them an anonymous
Christianity which they accept really, freely, in a subjectively
implicit way through their inner acquiescence in existence.

A *third* possibility: A person has anonymous Christianity
proffered to his freedom; he not only has it, he has also accepted it in the unreflexive spiritual acquiescence in existence.
In the depths of his being he freely believes. But on the level
of express, verbalized reflection he has heard nothing about
this Christianity. He is, for instance, somebody who, born
after 1918 and growing up in an officially bolshevist environment, has never, in a reflexive, express way, bothered about
religious problems or heard anything about them. Therefore
on the explicit, express level such a person has neither a
proffered nor a freely accepted Christianity, but on the anonymous, implicit level Christianity has not only been proffered to

him but has also been accepted by him with his own existence in an inner consent. Thus he has been invited and has personally and freely consented to be anonymously a Christian.

A *fourth* possibility: Here implicit, anonymously proffered Christianity is there only to the minimum extent in which it *cannot* be lacking. But out of hatred for his own existence the person in question rejects this innermost structure of his nature. He says No to it and to the whole of life. He does not want to believe in the hidden light. He refuses to surrender to this mystery of loving nearness which implicitly, anonymously permeates his existence. Such a case is possible. A person *can* in the uttermost depths of his being say No to his own being. Such a No is not merely a misunderstanding at the periphery of his reflexive consciousness. It can exist as the result of a free decision in the innermost core of the existence allotted to him by God, as a protest against God and against the loving nearness of the Mystery. Thus man can be the sinner, the unbeliever, deep down in himself. That such a case is possible is in itself a mystery, but it cannot be claimed that things never reach that pass. Theoretically it is possible that this anonymous proffered Christianity is actually present, but that the person freely, sinfully and culpably rejects it through his innermost rebellion against existence; hence that, in the ultimate and most radical meaning, he professes unbelief. Supposing, moreover, that this person, never having heard anything about Christianity on the level of reflection, was unable to arrive on this level either to a Yes or a No of reflex, express freedom; we would then have the most extreme form of unbelief in the proper sense of the word.

Of course, we may wonder whether such a theoretically constructed unbelief, occurring wholly in the unreflexive depths at the core of the person, totally beyond the reach of objectified, verbalized reflection, is really conceivable. This is subject to discussion. One might object that in every human being who has reached the age of reason, there is some objectively reflexive morality, be it ever so rudimentary. It need not necessarily be connected with an express religious theme in the strict sense of the word, but even so, to some extent some kind of express moral alternative is given. Take a man who has grown up in extreme bolshevism, who knows nothing about "God" on the explicit level of reflexively objective consciousness, to whom a real alternative for his free decision never occurs on that level. But even for him there are moral problems—whether concerning his conduct towards a party member he hates to denounce, even for his own advantage, or his conduct with respect to his wife and child. Here as everywhere—if it were only in the morality of thieves, who do not inform on each other—there are moral problems and alternatives which are presented to the reflexive, express decision of freedom.

But if it is difficult to admit that *only* an unreflexive, unthematic basic decision determines the religious and moral values of man, then factually and in practice such an unreflexive, unthematic basic decision for or against anonymous Christianity must always be accompanied by a reflexive, express, thematic free decision in this sense at least, that certain moral decisions of a reflexive nature are taken. To our table of possibilities, considered in a strictly formal sense, also belongs the case in which, on the level of explicit reflection, nothing of a religious nature is given—either as proffered or as freely acted upon—so that the decision occurs totally on the level of the unreflexive acceptance of existence. In this, our fourth possibility, anonymous Christianity is proffered to the person in question (as it is to every human being), but he has it in the context of hatred against himself, against existence, against God. In such a hatred he refuses it through a really free decision and makes this refusal and protest the specific content of his existence, even though perhaps in an anonymous, altogether unexplicit, manner.

A *fifth* possibility: A person has anonymous Christianity— as we have seen, one always has—but in his ultimate existential decision he rejects it. But here is where this possibility differs from the one we have described in the fourth place. He also has explicit possession of this Christianity which he rejects implicitly, and on the level of explicit reflection he accepts it. Take some average Christian. Christianity as inner grace, as inner dedication to God is, of course, proffered to him. And since he is an average Christian, he has also understood to some extent what he has been told about Christianity. We ask this man whether he believes what he has been told. Suppose now for this, our fifth possibility, that the person answers: Of course I believe, I belong to the Holy Name society, and I have never stopped fighting Communism. In a word, the man feels that he is an outstanding Christian. He may nevertheless be an unbeliever in the core of his person; he may say No in his unreflective attitude towards existence, rejecting anonymous Christianity as the divine self-donation in the depths of his being, although where this Christianity is given him explicitly he accepts it in that dimension. Hence Christianity of a verbalized, reflexive, ecclesiastical kind, explicitly presented and accepted, is still not an absolute criterion of the real acceptance of anonymously proffered Christianity in the core of the person. Someone may be an explicit Christian, and

yet on the anonymous level this Christianity proffered to him
may be rejected by the deepest free decision of his personality.
On this level he has Christianity only by way of a No.

Summarizing the possibilities we have considered, we may
say: Christianity may be accepted or rejected in the dimension
of reflection and in the dimension of the core of the person—
that is, as anonymous Christianity. We do not know with
absolute certitude which of the two attitudes prevails. We do
not even know this about ourselves, although we are explicitly
Christians. We do not know it in the case of others, even when
explicitly they are Christians. We do not know it at all for the
merely anonymous Christian, whose acceptance or rejection
is, of course, hidden in the depths of his being. What we know
is only that Christianity is anonymously given to everybody.
What we hope is that it exists in everybody as an inner consent, as personally appropriated in freedom. Everybody is allowed to hope this for all men, although only with more or
less probability of being right. Where coarseness and baseness
do not yield to any other influence and we must admit that
they are accepted in freedom, even there anonymous Christianity is still always proffered as an invitation. But there is not
much hope that cynicism and the denial of morality, a free
yielding to meaninglessness and the powers of darkness, will
not mean the rejection of this proffered anonymous Christianity. Whether this is truly so we know for certain in regard
to neither the "official" nor the common malefactors of world
history. On the other hand, we are equally uncertain whether
or not the upright and decent man, even when express and
conceptualized Christianity has been explicitly given to him,
implicitly denies it in unreflexive freedom.

By way of conclusion we may say: although the fact of

anonymous Christianity is a *universal possibility* of salvation —that is, one which is given to *every* human being—it is not an *assurance* of salvation. We may further say: the possibility of salvation is *Christian,* even when the person in question does not live within official, confessional, sociologically organized Christianity. Whether somebody, outside or inside official Christianity, accepts the possibility of salvation in freedom is a question whose answer remains the secret of God's judgment.

8 / The Relation Between Anonymous Christianity and Explicit Ecclesiastical Christianity

The theory of anonymous Christianity might give rise to the impression that reflexive Christianity—aware of itself, laid down in doctrines, and sociologically organized—that ecclesiastical Christianity all in all, is superfluous, or at least not very important. It might be wondered why we should try so hard and care so much about Christian education, Christian instruction and guidance, Christian missionary activity, if God has made man into a Christian from the start and the only thing that matters for salvation is the acceptance of oneself as such. Whether this or that person is a Christian of the anonymous kind or a professed Christian can be left to God, especially since we may really wonder whether the frenzy of organization, with its human—all too human—weaknesses does not perhaps produce the opposite effect, since it interferes, so to speak, with God's own activity. If we left everything to him, he would save man by taking hold of the innermost heart of his existence. Let us try to answer this objection.

We shall once more use the example of logic and consider

the relation between implicit and explicit logic. Say a man thinks logically, uses logical principles, perhaps even without reflection, in the end makes fewer mistakes in the logic of his practical conduct than the expert who can give erudite explanations of "logic." Does it follow, then, that since man can think and behave logically even without logic as an explicitly developed science, the science of logic as such is superfluous, a mere spiritual luxury? Or should we not say that an awareness of, a reflection upon, a structure of the human spirit which is exercised only in subjective implication, may at times be of essential significance? Take, for example, the man who professes absolute materialism. With all his materialism this man nevertheless thinks in a spiritual manner. Hence he must rise above what is purely material to a more sublime reality. Does this mean that his error in the reflexive sphere concerning the true nature of his spiritual existence has no bearing on the way he lives this spiritual existence? True, one who is a materialist on the level of reflection may talk as he will—this does not prevent him from living like a spiritual person. Nevertheless the error in which he is caught may induce him to perform actions which are against the nature of his spirit and hamper the implicit, anonymous, unreflexive development of his spiritual existence. Not in this sense, that because this man is convinced on the level of reflection that there is no morality he is absolutely unable to act morally. But one who simply rejects morality in his express thinking incurs by this explicit ethical error a real danger of admitting immorality freely in the depths of his being as well, of acting immorally in certain specific situations—deceiving his wife, or neglecting his children, or caring more for his own good than for that of others. He might not have acted immorally in this or that situation had it not been for this error, this idea that it does not really matter how all these material, chemical processes resolve themselves in his brain.

So there is a permanent interaction between the unreflexive, unthematic, anonymous domain on the one hand and the reflexive, thematic, verbalized domain on the other hand. We should not conceive these two domains as hermetically separated from each other. The implicit, the unreflexive continually permeates reflection, and reflection always reacts upon the unreflexive. It is undeniable, for instance, that a person may pray without knowing explicitly that he is praying. One who quietly, simply, in a matter-of-fact way and, as it were, for better or for worse, trustfully acquiesces in the unfathomable mystery of his existence, has done what we call "praying" even if he gives no name to this innermost reality of his existence or would be afraid of doing so. On the other hand, should we not add that such a prayer emerges more easily, that one prays more profoundly, more fully, in a way which permeates one's whole existence, when one has also learned to pray expressly, when reflexive and explicit prayer reverberates, as it were, in the hidden depths of one's being?

That is why we have said that the domains of the reflexive and unreflexive cannot be separated. The real, concrete, spiritual self-realization of man is constantly affected by this tension between the poles of the subjective and the objectively reflexive. To separate these two poles altogether would mean to suppress them completely. But granted that man has these two poles by his nature, it would contradict this spiritual nature if, on principle and from the start, we gave up any thematization of his anonymous unreflexive subjectivity. The only question, then, is to what extent the anonymity should become reflexive, to what extent this not expressly conscious morality, this name-less, mysterious character of existence, should be thematized. When people speak of love, gratitude, beauty, the world, or life, they do not thereby bring their spiritual existence into being, they simply bring to the light of express consciousness a spiritual existence which has been going on in the depths of their soul. This belongs to their essence as spiritual beings. Should we try to stop it and declare: "never again, let us leave these weighty subjects alone," the result would be that the anonymous, the subjective, the unreflexive would choke upon itself. True, one who evokes it never entirely catches up with it. In the innermost core of his being he always knows more than he can explicitate or others can tell him. No need of reading novels to know what love, gratitude, faithfulness, guilt or anxiety are. We know because we are living men, we know out of the subjectivity of our own being. Yet this does not prevent us from looking for the "poet," for the interpreter, who expresses, makes explicit, what we ourselves experience vaguely in the obscure depths of our being and all too frequently mis-understand.

What is true of all experience necessarily applies to this deepest experience of the life of the spirit which we call the religious experience. Like all other aspects of that life it needs to be expressed. It searches for self-interpretation and interpre-tation by others, since the intercommunication of men belongs to the essentials of existence. That is why the collective, social interpretation of what the individual experiences anonymously, unreflexively, is of paramount importance. That which is ex-perienced only anonymously would not remain alive if it did not meet in the other person the experience which he too has had. Only in personal exchange, in the I-Thou relationship,

does it stay alive and avoid the danger of choking on itself—
as joy would fade and never grow into real joy if it were not
also experienced by another, if it did not derive power and
influence from this sharing.

Even more decisive from the theological point of view is the
following consideration: God, as the Creator of "heaven" *and*
"earth," of the inner *and* the outer dimensions and possibilities
of man, wills, as a God of salvation, to be present in all these
dimensions of man. Not only, therefore, in the hidden personal
core of man, but also in his bodiliness, in the social, cultural,
ecclesial zone—in short, in every possible exteriorization in
word, gesture, work of art, and every activity. To exile God to
the mere interiority of a wordless, forever implicit conscience
or to subjective, mystical depths as the "proper place" of all
religion would be a profanation of all other dimensions of
human existence. Either this would imply that these dimensions of existence are indifferent for salvation—which they are
not and cannot be if there is really an intercommunication, an
interaction, an osmosis between the separate dimensions of
existence, and if the innermost zone is not a hermetically
isolated domain. Or such a relegation of God into the innermost conscience would mean that the other dimensions of
existence would have no connection with salvation, although
man is continually involved in them. This would be a dis-
figurement and a mutilation of man, since it would reduce him
to the domain of what is indifferent in itself and put beyond
his reach this dimension of real and eternal importance. God
would be exiled into some kind of no man's land.

This is certainly not the "anonymity" of which we have
been speaking. By its very definition it is the thing that comes
first, no matter when and how it will become explicit; it is a

promise and a task given by God, subject to the commanding will of God, the Lord of all the dimensions of human existence as well as of the innermost core of the person. This same divine will embodied his grace in the historical corporeity of Christ and called us to take a like way from the core of the hallowed person into the external manifestation of a Christianity formulated in concepts and organized along social and ecclesiastical lines. This is for us a duty whose actual fulfillment has a history directed by God and not only by us. As a result, God so willing or permitting, this development has not always and in all individuals moved equally far in the direction of that manifestation which we simply call Catholic Christianity.

"Men of Athens, I see that in every respect you are extremely religious. For as I was going about and observing objects of your worship, I found also an altar with this inscription: 'To the Unknown God.' What therefore you worship without knowing it, that I proclaim to you." (Acts 17: 22–23) These words of St. Paul to the Gentiles must be taken seriously and not interpreted too simply.

The doctrine of the "anonymous Christian" does not say any more than the Acts of the Apostles. It speaks of something that he does not know explicitly but nevertheless *knows;* otherwise he would not worship it. We are not trying to convince the anonymous Christian himself. The important point is first to convince the man whose Christianity is explicit. He should understand that the dilemma is not either to be optimistic in an unchristian way, by ascribing to these others an a-Christian possibility of salvation, which one should not ascribe to them, or to be pessimistic in an unchristian way by believing that there is no hope for their salvation. The Christian should understand that he does not have to be either optimistic or pessimistic in an unchristian way. Then he can behave more dispassionately and peacefully towards the world he experiences as an unbelieving world. He need no longer feel so directly threatened in his Christian existence by the presence of the innumerable multitude of "non-Christians." That is what really matters.

AFTERWORD:
THE ANONYMOUS CHRISTIAN
ACCORDING TO KARL RAHNER[1]

by Klaus Riesenhuber, S.J.

During the last few years the Church has become more deeply aware of her duty with respect to the world and of her openness towards the world. The Church welcomes contacts with other groups, Catholics engage in fraternal dialog with non-Catholics, in friendly collaboration with non-Christians. How shall we regard the non-Catholic partner in this collaboration, if it is not to remain merely an outward and illusory rapprochement and a superficial compromise? How can the person who does not profess Christianity have a share in Christ's salvation and thus ultimately stand in brotherly unity with us?

Shall we, in our pastoral message to modern man, present Christianity as a new exigency added on, one which strikes him, in the depths of his self-understanding, as something foreign and inaccessible? Or may Christian preaching rightfully start from the personal experience of a human being who is simply concerned with his own threatened existence? In the last analysis, isn't its goal simply to explain and interpret what every man has personally experienced, as "a theological depth-analysis of human consciousness, as it really is?"[2]

These questions constitute the theme of the present article.

It is Karl Rahner especially who has investigated this problem in several articles, although never directly. In her remarkable book *The Anonymous Christian* Anita Röper develops these basic ideas of Rahner. In her own personal way, without quotations or references to Rahner's writings, Frau Röper wishes to bring home to a "wider circle of readers"[3] a comprehension of anonymous Christianity. She does not presuppose in her readers a philosophical or theological background. This explains why her book places more stress on demonstrating the reality of an experience of God than on showing from theology that the anonymous Christian is really a Christian belonging to the Church.

Theological discussion stands in need of another work bringing together and organizing Rahner's ideas on the anonymous Christian, as they can be gathered from many scattered articles. Thus the present essay, which was written independently of the Röper book, tries, in strict fidelity to the sources, to present a systematic and comprehensive survey of the problem, so as to point out clearly its ontological and theological aspects. Because of the manysidedness of the problem many of these aspects can be indicated and justified only briefly, although they deserve a more extensive treatment and discussion than can be presented in these pages.

I. Starting Point and Statement of the Problem.

In order really to pinpoint what has been rather vaguely called the problem of "anonymous Christianity," we must state it clearly and make sure of a firm starting point. Thus the method, and by implication the goal, of our investigation will become apparent. As we may gather from the term "anonymous Christianity," we have to do here with a basic problem of theological anthropology[4] and ecclesiology. As a "Christian" the anonymous Christian has a positive relation to Christ, the redemption and his Church. But insofar as his Christianity is "anonymous," he does not belong, as a member, to the community of the visible Church which officially represents Christianity.

Hence the anonymous Christian belongs to that part of redeemed mankind which has not yet entered into the visible Church. That is how, as a starting point of our work, the "people of God" in the sense of objectively redeemed mankind[5] seems to present itself to us. But further epistemological and ontological reflection brings out the difficulties of this starting point. The inner structure of this people of God is not immediately given to us. Moreover, belonging to the people of God is only a preparation and a prerequisite for becoming a full-fledged Christian, it is a deficient modality of this process which can itself be fully understood only through its total development.

Hence the correct starting point lies in considering the end towards which mankind, in its supernatural finality, hence anonymous Christianity too, is directed on earth. If there is an anonymous Christianity, it must stand within the dynamism towards this end of God's salvific activity. But what is directed towards an end has also been designed by this end as by its final cause and can be fully understood only in terms of it.

In explaining this end, we shall not start from any specific point of the faith—be it ever so central, like the Incarnation—but from the consciousness which the Christian has of his faith. In this consciousness we discover not only the several dogmas of the faith, at least implicitly, but also something of the concrete, non-verbalizable, experience and interpretation

of what it means to be a human being and a Christian.[6] We
must clarify this consciousness with regard to the question of
the end of mankind. From this statement of the end, whose
validity may be checked against the pronouncements of the
Church, we shall deduce the prerequisites which are necessarily
given together with this end—when God wills the end, he also
wills the means required for it. Finally, within the framework
of the anthropology which we shall thus have sketched, we
shall weigh the possibility of anonymous Christianity.

   The Christian knows that God has spoken to him in history
freely and through grace, that he has revealed himself to him
and that this revelation is not reserved only for him but must
reach all men.[7] God reveals himself to mankind in the Incarnation of Christ, whose meaning and purpose is therefore
the self-communication of God to the whole of humanity.[8]
The Incarnation is an inner moment and a condition of the
possibility of the radical self-manifestation of God to mankind.
God's grace, which radiates from the historical center of the
Incarnation, is assimilated by peoples and individuals in a
historical process. In accordance with the bodily[9] and the
sociological[10] structure of man and on account of the incarnational, sacramental and ecclesial character of the grace of
Christ[11] this process naturally consists in becoming a member
of the visible, juridically organized Church of Christ. The
"mystery . . . of the Church is but an extension of the mystery
of Christ."[12] Hence the purpose of God's salvific activity on
earth is the visible Church.

   But the Church is neither formally nor materially identical
with this mankind which is called to salvation. Rather, as a
signum elevatum in nationes,[13] it is separated from the rest of
mankind. Therefore membership in the Church depends on

peculiar conditions which derive from the nature of the Church. In agreement with the differentiated, pluralistic character of the Church, there are different degrees of membership in it.[14] But as we dispose of only one word ("member" or "non-member") it follows that "when we use this word, it is also a question of terminology where . . . we shall put the boundary line between member and non-member. It is up to the Church to determine the usage of the term."[15] Within the basic structure and function of the Church as the place where salvation is bestowed and as the visible embodiment of God's salvific will in history,[16] the Church herself may lay down the conditions of membership, and she may even do this in different ways at different times. Thus subjection to the Church through baptism may be conceived as a kind of membership.[17] But full juridical membership depends on the reception of baptism, on the confession of the Catholic faith and on union with the Church and her hierarchy.[18] A membership which is complete from every point of view—over and above the mere juridical, visible aspect—is to be found only in "the believing and obedient Catholic who lives in the state of justifying grace."[19] Even if we adopt the widest conception of membership, the majority of men remain outside the Church.

But the Church is not, as shown above, a fortuitous, purely human association of people who would already have been redeemed before she came into existence; it is rather the place where salvation is bestowed, since all salvation is of Christ and therefore of his Church. Hence the question of Church membership is not only of canonical interest, but is also of existential import. According to the utterances of the magisterium, as summarized in the axiom *Extra Ecclesiam nulla salus* (outside the Church no salvation), belonging to the visible Church is necessary for salvation.[20] This necessity of belonging to the Church must be understood as a necessity of means, as a *necessitas medii,* not simply as a *necessitas praecepti* (a necessity of precept).[21] Hence even in case of need, it cannot simply be replaced by man's good will.

But the Christian does not only know of the necessity for salvation of membership in the Church, he also knows of God's universal salvific will.[22] It is for him an existential necessity to profess belief in God's salvific will for all men if he is to believe in God's salvific will for himself.[23]

Thus we have discovered the end of God's salvific activity —the salvation of all men through their belonging to the Church. But the conditions for membership in the Church and historical circumstances do not at present make it possible for all men to be members of the Church. Therefore God's universal salvific will demands that a way should exist of belonging to the Church which does not entail full-fledged membership. What can we say about the nature and the requirements of such a possibility of salvation which might be found in a non-official and incomplete way of belonging to the Church?

Man is not simply justified by the grace of God, but specifically by the grace of Christ.[24] Hence everyone who is justified through faith must also be oriented towards Christ and his grace, and thus also towards the Church of Christ . . . "if it is true . . . that salvation . . . is Christ's salvation, since there is no other salvation, then it must be possible for someone to be not only an anonymous theist, but also an anonymous Christian."[25] Anonymous Christianity presupposes and includes a belonging to the Church or an orientation towards her. But as this Church is a visible Church, this belonging to her must also be visible. A mere inward *votum Ecclesiae* (desire for the Church) does not seem to be enough for the dogma of the necessity for salvation of the visible Church.[26]

Thus a consideration of the end of salvation has clearly outlined the problem of our essay: How is it possible that human beings who have never heard of salvation in Christ and of his Church may nevertheless believe in Christ and be visibly oriented towards his Church? In order to answer this question, we shall first deduce from the end of the work of salvation, as explained above, the necessary presuppositions of this end in the natural and supernatural domains. Next we shall try to show how man in his self-realization necessarily assumes a certain position with respect to these presuppositions, which are transcendentally prior to his free decision, and can thus orient himself through a personal decision towards Christ and his Church, even in a visible manner. If we succeed in doing this, we shall have established the possibility and the foundation of anonymous Christianity.[27]

II. The Ontological Constitution of Those Who Are Called to Salvation

The Christian conceives of himself as someone who, as a creature and a sinner, has been invited into God's own most inward life by God and by the active word of his free, absolute self-manifestation.[28] God reveals himself to man freely, without inner or outer necessity. As a free and autonomous person God cannot be grasped from without; he is not forced to manifest himself. If God manifests himself to man, this can happen only in free spontaneity.[29] This is true not only because man is a sinner and has forfeited his rights, not only because God has freely created man. Rather, revelation, as a mutual personal relationship, as a dialog between God and man, presupposes its recipient,[30] in such a manner that, even for its pre-existing recipient, it remains a free favor of God. Only in this way can there be a real dialog. Thus the essence of revelation supposes in man a stable, self-subsistent nature, which is given prior to any revelation, which in no way implies or unconditionally demands revelation. It follows that this nature of man must continue to exist irrespective of whether God reveals himself or man rejects God's self-communication.[31] On the other hand, it follows for revelation and the supernatural order that, unlike pure nature, they are not transcendentally affirmed in their denial and their rejection.[32]

Of what kind must this human nature be in order to be a possible recipient and bearer of God's revelation and self-communication? How does the nature of man look to us empirically?

If nature is to be capable of receiving God in his radical self-communication, it must stand in an infinite openness and transcendence towards the unlimited being, hence towards God. In a word, this nature must be a spirit. The condition of the possibility of receiving grace is a nature's spirituality: ". . . the transcendental presence of . . . the infinite mystery (called God) [is] the basis for a possible movement (through that which we call God's self-communication in grace) aiming at the immediate vision of God."[33] Hence the capacity for receiving revelation, the *potentia obedientialis,* is not one capacity in man among many others, it is the spirit opening up towards infinity, hence human nature itself.[34] We are able to meet the world in knowledge and volition because of the unlimited horizon of our spirit, which reaches out for the infinity of God in and through and across every single object, even though this reaching out and its object are conscious only in an unobjective, transcendental way.[35] This reaching out, this dynamism, which constitutes the essence of the finite spirit, puts man in the expectation of a revelation and in a basic readiness for God's self-communication.[36] Insofar as this reaching out tends dynamically towards the infinite, we can also legitimately speak of a positive (albeit a conditional, see below pp. 157f.) finality of man towards the reception of supernatural grace.[37] Within the history of philosophy we owe the development of this point to the school of Maréchal, in which the apparently minor theorem of the *desiderium naturale visionis beatificae* as found in the doctrine of St. Thomas became "the central and essential idea for our understanding of a spiritual nature."[38]

If we have thus discovered in man a finality towards God and his revelation—hence also an opening for the "anonymous theist" and for the believer in a possible revelation—we must now inquire theologically whether it is not also possible to discover in man a finality towards Christ, God incarnate, or a specific tendency towards the knowledge of Christ: . . . the fact of Christ's existence is the most free, and in this sense (but also only in this sense) the most 'fortuitous' fact of reality; it is also both the most decisive and the most important fact, and the one with the most evident reference to man (. . . *propter nos homines,* for us men). It is impossible simply to take his subjective cognoscibility for granted as one of the data of a general critique or metaphysics of knowledge. He is too wholly unique, too mysterious, too existentially important for this."[39]

What can the Incarnation of the Logos tell us about human

nature? "Is the humanity of the Logos merely something ex-
traneous which has been assumed, or is it precisely the thing
that originates when the Logos utters himself into that which
is not God?"[40] When we seriously believe that the Logos *becomes* man—and not merely that a human nature begins to
subsist in him—when the man Jesus is really a visible appearance of God amongst men, then Christ's humanity is not something designed prior to the idea of the Incarnation and independently of it, "but that which comes into being and takes
shape as a possibility and as a reality when, and insofar as,
the Logos empties himself. The man Jesus is, precisely as man,
the self-expression of God in his self-emptying, since God expresses himself precisely when he empties himself."[41] But as
our human nature is equal to Christ's human nature in its
quiddity (that which makes a thing what it is),[42] it follows
that human nature as such is the possible self-expression of the
self-emptying God.[43] Thus "man as originally defined is: the
possible externalization of God in his self-emptying and the
possible brother of Christ."[44] If the *potentia obedientialis* for
the hypostatic union and for grace (the grace of Christ) are
not a potency *beside* others, but constitute man's very nature. . . , and if the latter (nature equals *potentia obedientialis*), something which is far from self-evident, can be known
from its act, it can manifest itself in fullest clarity and reveal
its real mystery only in its highest act, which consists in being
the otherness of God himself" (*das Andere Gottes selbst*).[45]
Hence a complete, self-contained anthropology is impossible
unless it includes Christology; likewise in the elaboration of
dogmatic theology, Christology finds its most appropriate
place in anthropology, since otherwise Christology can only
with difficulty avoid the semblance of mythology.[46]

We have grasped all this "from above," from the fact of God's self-emptying; it should now be possible to demonstrate it also from below, from the specific nature and the ultimate dynamism of human nature (even though such a presentation has become possible for us only because we already know of the reality of the Incarnation).[47] If it belongs to man's nature to be oriented beyond himself towards the mystery of God, not in such a way as to comprehend the mystery, but to be comprehended and ordered by it; if, in its original ground, human nature is "the self-aware orientation of emptiness towards this fullness"[48] of God, then we may say that in this nature and its self-transcendence the first outline and idea of its adoption by God himself, hence also the idea of a God-man, is already pre-designed.[49] "It is the meaning of this nature . . . to be that which is given away, surrendered; to be that which reaches its perfection and comes to itself by disappearing for itself permanently in the Unknowable. . . . Hence the Incarnation of God is the unique, supreme instance of the total self-fulfillment of human reality, which consists in this: that man *is* by giving himself away."[50] Thus a real experience and knowledge of human nature shows "that there is an . . . idea of the God-man which is given together with the essence of man and of his self-transcendence."[51]

Thus the ultimate, distant goal of human nature is its fulfillment as the otherness of God.[52] This possibility and finality on the part of human nature cannot be interpreted as coinciding by chance with God's supernatural salvific design. The nature must rather be understood as that which God presupposes for himself so as to enter into it in self-emptying and self-communication, so as to become it.[53] Hence God's self-communication is what is basically and primarily intended by

him, and this will of God presupposes man in his nature as a
necessary means for this self-communication.[54] But for God the
whole of creation is presupposed as a condition for the possibility of man. Thus—when we look at it from the point of
view of the effect—the cosmos has its purpose in man, the
latter finds his fulfillment in the reception of grace,[55] of which
the Incarnation is a condition and a constitutive element:[56]
Incarnation and a humanity enriched by grace are "ontologically . . . the undeniable purpose of creative activity as a
whole."[57]

If we probe even deeper, we can not only say that God's
real creative action is an intermediate step (*die Vermittlung*)
for his self-emptying,[58] but that even the possibility of creation
is based on the possibility of the self-communication of God,
so that God's creative power must be understood as the "derived, circumscribed, secondary possibility"[59] as compared
with the primary initial possibility of his self-communication
to the other.[60] Thus the creature is "always [projected] as the
grammar of a possible self-utterance"[61] of God, hence dis-
posed in view of this self-utterance and its expectation.

Do these insights into the natural capability and orientation
of the creature with respect to God's self-communication not
do away with the strictly supernatural, gratuitous and unforeseeable character of God's self-revelation? Do they not
contradict our previous idea, that by its very nature revelation must be some kind of dialog—hence free, not brought
about by force, wholly gratuitous? When we deduce the possibility of an incarnation of God from nature, are we not trying
to restrict the unlimited range of God's possibilities, to determine and thus to circumscribe the Incarnation previous to
its realization?

We reply that the possibility of the Incarnation has not been deduced purely apriori. Before Christ no attempt was made to outline an Incarnation as a possibility. But now the philosopher not only stands in the clear light of Christ's grace, he also knows Christ by the spoken word of revelation, "and it [would be] a mistake . . . to believe that we can—even in a purely methodical way—totally abstract from him."[62] Nowadays the questions the philosopher asks and the horizon against which he thinks are unavoidably influenced by his knowledge of the Incarnation. Thus considering the Incarnation as a possibility does not mean that we derive it from our own mind, but only that we rediscover reflectively, autonomously, what has already been given to us.

Moreover, the *potentia obedientialis* of human nature for the supernatural may be conceived as a positive orientation towards grace without destroying the free gratuitousness of the supernatural.[63] To understand the *potentia obedientialis* as a mere absence of contradiction in the relation between nature and grace would lead to an extrinsicism of grace.[64] God's self-manifestation remains free if it neither follows with necessity merely from God's nature nor can be demanded as a right by the creature. As a free person, God does not have to reveal himself.[65] The creature's finality towards God's self-communication would, as a potency, demand its fulfillment through grace only if it should be meaningless without such a reception of grace.[66] But, as has been shown, the *potentia obedientialis* is identical with man's spiritual nature, and its reaching for transcendence is the condition for the possibility of the spirit's encounter with the world, and thus for the self-perfecting of the person, which constitutes an absolute value.[67]

Thus the transcending dynamism of man has a meaning even if it is not perfected by grace, so that the reception of grace cannot be demanded on its account.[68] Finally, should God not reveal himself, the openness of man for God's transcendence would still have a positive meaning: man would note the very silence of God,[69] which is also a free action of his with respect to his creature, and thus a kind of communication.[70] Thus it can be seen that the reception of grace and "the hypostatic union are the most radical way in which a created spirit transcends itself, . . . a way which cannot be reached by the creature of itself, and one which, nevertheless, fulfills in an eminent manner the nature of the creature's transcendence."[71]

We can briefly summarize what we have said thus far. By his very nature man is conditionally oriented towards God, his revelation and his self-communication in the God-man.

God has freely and definitively promised himself to man. He has put man under the obligation of reaching his supernatural fulfillment as the only end which must absolutely be reached. This supernatural destination freely imparted to man cannot be only a design hidden in God, which could be known to man only through spoken revelation. On the contrary, the will of God which decides thus about the creature takes shape in this creature, it becomes a real-ontological determination of the creature's condition (not of its nature). That which God demands from the world is, as its unconditional orientation towards this exigency, the world's real character.[72] Hence the orientation of the world towards the supernatural end does not consist merely in a juridical obligation, in a *ens juridicum*.[73] To say this would be nominalism.[74] It constitutes rather a reality of the human condition, a prior datum of man's free activity and of his justification, which may be called the supernatural "existential."[75] This "existential" is supernatural and gratuitous because it is not already given with nature (i.e., nature as opposed to grace, to the supernatural),[76] but is freely imparted to man by God. As a continuation, as a deepening interiorization, of the *potentia obedientialis,* this supernatural "existential" can not be understood as a quality which, as supernatural, only touches the periphery of nature without affecting it inwardly; it is "that which is innermost in man."[77] That which is uppermost is also innermost. The whole final dynamism of nature is concentrated in this real supernatural destination of man; it is tied up with the supernatural end, and thus called permanently and really to rise above itself, so that it can no longer, without loss of balance, "shut itself up within its own ambit."[78] Thus the concept of the supernatural "existential" helps us understand how a gift which is contingent with respect to man's nature, as is the Incarnation and the vocation to grace, may become absolutely decisive for the interpretation of man and his destiny,[79] because this gift at once elevates and summarizes this nature.

The supernatural "existential" cannot be refused by man; it is given to him, whether he accepts or rejects the gift of grace, along with his nature.[80] Inasmuch as man's whole nature is permeated by it and culminates in it, the person who rejects his supernatural vocation stands with his whole being in the shadow of doom and is unable to keep any remnant of his nature sound and unscathed.[81] Likewise the *poena damni* (punishment of damnation) can be explained only in terms of an unconditional orientation of the whole person to the love of

God as a source of grace; hence in terms of the supernatural "existential."[82]

Hence man is ordered unconditionally towards a strictly supernatural life in grace as his final end. This grace, if it is to be wholly supernatural, hence not connatural to a single creature,[83] must consist in the uncreated grace; therefore, in the self-communication of God.[84] But this self-communication of God can be accepted by man as a strictly supernatural communication—that is as a divine *self*-communication—only if its very acceptance by man is already the work of (created) grace. In order to remain divine, not to be weakened and limited, circumscribed by the inner world of the finite recipient, the self-communication must presuppose created grace as a material disposition, so that its acceptance may be the work of this grace.[85] This grace, which, owing to God's universal salvific will, must be proffered to every man,[86] is best understood not as merely an occasional, intermittent intervention of God, but more correctly as something which is permanently offered to a human being in his moral freedom. Thus the supernatural horizon of transcendence towards the God of grace stands permanently open for man as he is enveloped by God's salvific will taking concrete shape in the offer of grace.[87] This proffered grace, which enables man adequately to accept the God who communicates himself in word and action, already contains in itself some kind of (inner, not public) revelation.[88] Thus man lives within the range of God's salvific will revealing itself in the tender of grace.

In the above presentation of a theological anthropology we considered mainly the individual and transcendental aspect of man, but not the embodiment of these essential features in what is categorically visible and social. Although this other aspect of human nature contributes much to a complete survey of Christian anthropology, we cannot consider it here, not only for lack of space, but also because these essential characteristics of man do not have a decisive importance for anonymous Christianity. The anonymous Christian is precisely the person who already shares Christ's salvation inwardly, without being as yet able to bring this sharing to its full categorical embodiment and development.

With the foregoing explanations we have set forth those essential elements of man in the present order of salvation which at the same time constitute the possible basis for at least an anonymous Christianity. Man is a being who opens up towards God's transcendence; consequently, towards the possible God-man and the grace brought by him. His conditional orientation towards God's self-communication has been raised by God's free action to the level of an unconditional finality towards grace. This unconditional orientation of man towards grace is met by the permanent tendering of grace by God, which finds its meaning in the preparation of man for the reception of God's self-communication. This whole complex reality of man, as we have considered it thus far, is God's work of ordering and disposing, done prior to man's free decision. Hence it belongs to what is known in modern terminology as "nature"[89] (as opposed not to grace and the supernatural, but to "person"). We must now see to what extent man, as he develops into a person who disposes freely of himself, can assume a position with respect to these constitutive elements of his nature and thus be able, even without spoken revelation and sacraments, to decide for Christianity, albeit only its anonymous form.[90]

*III.　The Self-Realization of the Person and the
Possibility of Anonymous Christianity*

Since man is a free spiritual being, the nature which is handed over to his free self-determination requires that he shall accept it freely, realize and shape it personally. Man is able to shape his nature in this way, as the source of his actions, because the spirit, when reaching out towards its objects, turns back on itself, is present to itself.[91] Every spiritual act is essentially retroverted to the subject; that is why it possesses consciousness and why it imparts light and awareness to the substance. The spiritual act is not a "sporadically occurring concern of man with an object distinct from him . . . a transitory activity leaving the acting subject as such unaffected"[92]; it is, on the contrary, the initial self-realization (*Selbstvollzug*) of the substance. Thus a free decision does not merely refer to an outside object, but through it the subject determines himself in his innermost center, while entering into relation with something outside himself.[93] "Hence the free decision tends to affect the acting subject in his entirety."[94] Therefore one who through a free decision says Yes to himself, thus accepting himself, accepts his whole given nature at once with all its structures, "accepts himself in the immeasurable reaches of his unpredictable destiny,"[95] although he does not fully succeed in this in every single decision.[96] But this transcendental function of freedom operates only through man's intercourse with the world, through the categorical aspect of freedom. Nevertheless, the self-realization of freedom may originate from every datum of this world.[97]

What happens, on closer examination, when the subject accepts and determines himself? What realities are affected in this transcendental freedom of choice? Since in self-acceptance a choice is involved which also implies the possibility of shutting oneself off and rejecting oneself, the object of the choice must in some way be known, be within the domain of consciousness; a reality that is totally unknown does not come within the range of freedom.[98] The essential features given to man as his nature are true ontological realities, not merely *entia juridica* (juridical beings)—which could not, of course, appear before consciousness through their reality.[99] Moreover, every reality is self-present, hence conscious, in proportion to its degree of being. This applies especially to the spirit and all its natural and supernatural determinations.[100] It follows that we can say already, apriori, that such realities as the openness to transcendence, the supernatural "existential" and proffered grace must in some way be conscious, hence necessarily subject to man's free decision.

We must now demonstrate this in detail aposteriori also, on the basis of man's personal experience. It should be noted that in this experience the different realities are not given as clearly distinguishable from each other. Man's nature, his spirit, are totally interfused with his supernatural vocation, elevated by proffered grace, so that the immediate data are only the differently accentuated and graded experiences of the one concrete human life.[101] Hence, in order to discover what is given in these experiences we must also have recourse to apriori considerations.

Where do we find in man experiences which are sustained by the supernatural?[102] There is "the experience of infinite nostalgia, of radical optimism, of unquenchable dissatisfaction; the torment arising from the insufficiency of all tangible things, the deeply felt protest against death; the experience of encountering an absolute love even where it appears in utter incomprehensibility and seems to shroud itself in silence; the sense of a radical guilt paired, nevertheless, with a firm hope, and so on."[103] All these more striking experiences are ultimately but specific manifestations of the one basic experience, that man lives in and from the mystery, is rooted in it, is surrounded and invited by it.[104]

Such knowledge of the mystery reveals the openness to transcendence proper to the nature of the spirit, its orientation to God, perhaps more precisely to God as father,[105] which, as the precondition of all objective knowledge and volition, is unobtrusively but inevitably co-conscious.[106] Likewise every recognition of an absolutely obligatory "ought" carries with it by necessary implication a recognition of God in his absolute value and his creative volition, even where explicitly all knowledge of God is denied.[107]

Therefore one who readily accepts his own natural transcendence, who yields with docility to the mystery, who, in his moral activity, welcomes the call of God showing himself in the mystery, has hereby already accepted God, even when this knowledge remains implicit and perhaps he considers himself an atheist.[108] Insofar as this experience of transcendence is based on the natural dynamism of the spirit, it remains purely natural, it is not yet faith, it possesses no power to justify. But the idea permits us to conceive the possibility of the anonymous theist.

But actual self-experience does not stop at the experience of natural transcendence, it also contains an experience of grace. This must be shown in greater detail.

The problem of the experience of grace[109] should not be confused with the problem of the certitude of justification and salvation. For the experience of grace does not necessarily yield any certitude concerning the free acceptance of this grace, especially since "experience and reflexive experience are not the same thing."[110]

If man as a spirit is endowed with a finality to the supernatural end, this "existential" is the highest destination of his spirit. Because of its high ontological level and its inherence in the spirit it must itself be conscious.[111] We reach the same conclusion when we realize that the grace offered to man is divinizing grace, which already carries within itself the beginning of the *visio beatifica:*[112] such a grace cannot be entirely beyond the realm of consciousness.[113] Another approach leads to the same conclusion: the natural experience of transcendence is based upon the natural formal object of the spirit, which, as horizon, is co-conscious in every natural act of knowing and willing and which determines natural knowledge and volition in their basic structure and ontological value. But a supernatural act cannot be reached by any natural elevation of the natural faculties. It lies instead on a level which is essentially different ontologically. Hence it cannot be contained within a spiritual formal object which is purely natural; otherwise it would itself necessarily become a natural act. Thus the supernatural act needs its own supernatural formal object which, as a spiritual formal object, is conscious,[114] although not known as an object.[115]

This supernatural formal object, which necessarily accompanies the supernatural "existential," cannot be objectivated, cannot be simply grasped by reflexive consciousness, since, as horizon, it is the condition of the possibility of objective knowledge, hence in itself forever beyond such knowledge. Hence in reflection it cannot be clearly distinguished from

other data of consciousness, especially from the natural formal
object, since it does not appear to us as supernatural: the
experience of grace does not necessarily imply the experience
of grace as grace or the experience of grace as a content which
can be contrasted with natural data.[116] Although the experience of grace is unobjective in itself, it will produce in consciousness effects which may be observed reflexively.[117] Thus,
for instance, when concupiscence is experienced as something
alien to man, as something which ought not to be, this experience is based on a comparison of concupiscence with experienced grace; for in itself it is in accord with nature, but it
conflicts with grace and with the connatural effects of grace.[118]

The grace which is proffered to man and experienced by
him cannot be understood simply as a complement or counter-
part of the spoken revelation of certain truths by God. We
should rather say that, as God's word itself is already fraught
with grace, so his grace is "vocal," is revealing. Thus communication of grace is, in reality, always also revelation of
dogma to the individual. Thus "this reality which is presented
by the historic and public message of revelation may also be
given and experienced in the religious experience of the person
living in grace existentially, 'from within.' "[119] What is an-
nounced throughout revelation is ultimately nothing but the
divinizing bestowal of grace upon man through the self-
communication of the triune God. It is precisely this bestowal
of grace which is experienced by man, so that the content of
revelation is already given to man before he hears its message
spoken. Hence we may say that in the grace through which
God enables man to listen to revelation in the right way "he
(communicates) the reality of that . . . of which he speaks in
the word of revelation. Therefore spoken revelation about

some reality occurs in the present instance only in the communication by grace of the revealed reality itself; revelation merely explains that reality and brings it into objective consciousness."[120] The revealed content of Christianity does not come to man wholly from without in such a way that he finds within himself no affinity with it. It is already immanent to man as he lives in the concrete order of salvation; the "three absolute mysteries of Christianity (Trinity, Incarnation, Grace) are . . . experienced, as man is aware of himself as inevitably grounded in the abyss of the unfathomable mystery and experiences this mystery in the depth of his conscience and in the concrete details of his history . . . as a beneficent intimacy and not as a searing judgment."[121]

This experience of grace, which extends all the way up to an experience of the Trinity,[122] presupposes and has its foundation in man's nature as he experiences it. For by his very nature man is the capacity for "pure surrender of the inquiry-about-the-mystery to this mystery"[123] and knows himself as such. Thus the possibility of an incarnation and a bestowal of grace belongs to the truths which are already faintly delineated "in the pure mystery of the primordial understanding of man."[124] And Christianity is "nothing but . . . the clear expression of what man experiences vaguely in his concrete existence,"[125] "that which is divinely simple and supremely matter-of-course."[126]

If revelation and proffered grace are present in every man, he can also, in a personal way, realize and accept them. For every free act of the spirit has a tendency to permeate the whole person. If grace and the revelation contained in it were wholly unconscious, they would lie outside the range of a possible human choice or decision. Since, however, they are conscious as unobjective horizon and as inner dynamism, it is possible for man, in his encounter with the world, either to reject or to accept this inner revelation.[127] If man accepts God's revelation in the grace proffered to him, he makes a supernatural act of faith.[128] But man accepts revelation when he fully accepts himself, since revelation is deposited in himself. The act of faith which is thus made is, as *fides implicita* (implicit faith)—which is akin to Straub's *fides virtualis*[129]— undeveloped, hardly conscious as such. Nevertheless, because it is rooted in the supernatural formal object in which every available empirical reality is experienced,[130] it can be the basis and the substratum of all explicitly conscious volition and action; it can permeate this volition supernaturally, thus making of the person one who is already justified in a hidden way, an anonymous Christian. "One who fully accepts the fact of being man . . . has accepted the Son of man,"[131] because "the center of man is God himself and his form is the form of God incarnate himself."[132]

Thus "the silent gentleness of patience in the performance of one's daily duty"[133] may be the way in which many a "pagan" accepts himself, and thereby God. Likewise the constant preference given to the good in any particular sphere of morals may be a sign that such a man has decided definitely for the good and thus for the God of revelation.[134] Finally, man may also decide for the God of eternal life by going with faith and with hope through the act of dying, by which he lets himself be drawn into the abyss of the meaningful mystery.[135]

God bestows upon man the grace of Christ.[136] This grace is the grace of Christ not only owing to its origin—or else in itself nothing would be active or visible without this origin—but also on account of its inner reality; it really carries in itself the marks of Christ's salvific activity. Since the Church is "but the extension of the mystery of Christ,"[137] the grace of Christ too is always already ecclesiological in its nature,[138] related to the Church and referring to the Church. Thus the acceptance of grace in faith contains the source of an inner dynamism towards the Church. Hence this yearning for the Church is based not only on the natural tendency to a socialization, even in the religious domain,[139] nor only on the positive will of Christ—this would presuppose explicit knowledge through spoken revelation—but on the objective structure of grace, making itself felt existentially, in a conscious manner.[140] Therefore one who has existentially accepted grace is heading towards the Church, possesses a *votum implicitum* (implicit desire) for membership in the Church.

Like every free, personal act, faith too—and thus also the accompanying desire for membership in the Church—strives to assume embodiment and visible presentation. Although the free decision can not be equated with its bodily expression—the two do not even develop in a strictly parallel way[141]—there is no free decision which does not somehow permeate the bodily sector and express itself in it. Man "is not a personal spirit 'plus' a bodily being. Bodiliness is rather the necessary and only way in which he can actualize his spiritual being."[142] The free act incarnates itself[143] in its counterpole, which derives from man's own spiritual nature, thus incarnates itself in bodiliness.[144] To this ontological structure of the recipient of grace corresponds the structure of grace itself. As the grace of the Incarnate God it is incarnational and sacra-

mental,[145] it necessarily brings about its visible expression.
Hence there is no such thing as a purely internal act of faith
or a purely internal desire for the Church. Because it is a free
act of the spirit, the desire for the Church is also bodily and
visible.[146] The desire of a human being for the Church has,
with ontological necessity, a visible expression as a constitutive sign. This does not mean, however, that it can without
further ado be gathered from the outward appearance of such
a person. " 'Expression' and 'sign' imply an ontological quality
of the human act in its relation to grace and to the Church,
not a gnoseological quality aimed at any conceivable cognitive
power."[147]

Justification and the historico-social manifestation of salvation—through the visible bond with the Church—constitute
in their original and in their complete development a real
unity; although they do not simply coincide and may even
grow at different rates,[148] they can never be completely separated from each other. Rather, we have seen that even on the
lowest level—the level of the anonymous Christian—they are
tied to each other.[149] In this way the axiom *Extra Ecclesiam
nulla salus,* which refers to the visible Church, receives a correct interpretation, insofar as all salvation implies a visible
bond with the Church—even though not yet a membership in
it. Hence the doctrines of God's universal salvific will and the
necessity of the Church as a means of salvation do not contradict each other.[150]

The conclusion reached by our essay is this: when a person
in his own self-realization welcomes and lives up to what is
given to him by his nature and craves actualization; when,
moreover, he does not know (or not know enough) of spoken

revelation, and is thus deprived of a real access to the sacraments and to the official Church, the result is an anonymous Christian.

We can mention only briefly the practical consequences of the foregoing considerations. If we have good reasons for supposing that the grace of Christ is already at work everywhere, Christianity no longer looks like one religion among many others, but like their perfection, their secret entelechy, and also their judge.[151] Then the widespread absence of Christianity throughout the world is no longer so overwhelming to us,[152] because we can already see, even in one who is publicly a non-Christian, the anonymous Christian[153] who may, deep down in his heart, share the same faith and the same grace as the churchgoing Christian. In this way the juridically organized Church may be understood not as the exclusive community of those who are saved, but rather as the visible vanguard of Christians.[154]

This also shows us how important the visible image of the Church is.[155] In this conception the obligation of the apostolate and of incorporating the pagans into the Church continues to exist in its full rigor. For the Church presents greater possibilities of salvation than those available in the implicit state of anonymous Christianity. Moreover, the Church is not only a means of salvation but its visible presentation. It is only by incorporating the pagans that she reaches her fullness. And the grace imparted to the pagans yearns for its fulfillment in the Church.[156] Thus the apostolate is the endeavor to bring the Christianity which is already prefigured in every human being, and often actualized, to its full development and its reflexive self-awareness.[157]

Notes

1 The background for the philosophical part of the work is consti-
tuted by Karl Rahner's *Geist in Welt,* Munich, 2d ed. (1957) and
Hörer des Wortes, Munich, 2d ed. (1963), quoted as H.d.W.
The immediate sources for the present work are:
(1) Karl Rahner, *Theological Investigations,* Baltimore, Vols. I–II
(1961–1963); *Schriften zur Theologie,* Vols. III-V (1956–
1962).
From these volumes the following articles have been considered:
Vol. I: Current Problems in Christology. Theological Reflections on Monogenism. Concerning the Relationship between
Nature and Grace. Some Implications of the Scholastic Con-
cept of Uncreated Grace. The Theological Concept of *Con-
cupiscentia.*
Vol. II: Membership of the Church According to the Teach-
ing of Pius XII's Encyclical "Mystici Corporis Christi." The
Dignity and Freedom of Man. Guilt and Its Remission: the
Borderland between Theology and Psychotherapy.
Vol. III: Die ewige Bedeutung der Menschheit Jesu für
unser Gottesverhältnis. Über die Erfahrung der Gnade. Der
Christ und seine ungläubigen Verwandten. Über Konversionen.
Vol. IV: Über den Begriff des Geheimnisses in der katho-
lischen Theologie. Bemerkungen zum dogmatischen Traktat
De trinitate. Zur Theologie der Menschwerdung. Natur une
Gnade.
Vol. V: Über die Möglichkeit des Glaubens heute. Welt-
geschichte und Heilsgeschichte. Das Christentum und die
nichtchristlichen Religionen. Das Christentum und der "neue
Mensch." Die Christologie innerhalb einer evolutiven Weltan-
schauung. Einige Bemerkungen über die Frage der Konversionen. Dogmatische Randbemerkungen zur Kirchenfrömmig-
keit.
Both the English *Theological Investigations* (Vols. I and II)
and the as yet untranslated *Schriften zur Theologie* (Vols. III,
IV and V) are quoted simply by volume and page. Thus II 81
means *Theological Investigations,* Vol. II, page 81. And IV
319 means *Schriften zur Theologie,* Vol. IV, p. 319.

(2) The following articles by Karl Rahner in the *Lexikon für Theologie und Kirche* (abbreviated as LThK), 2nd ed. Freiburg, Vol. I (1957)-Vol. VIII (1963):
Altes Testament. *Anima naturaliter christiana.* Anthropologie. Atheismus. Christentum. Heidentum. Heiligmachende Gnade. Heilssorge. Heilswille. Katholizismus. Kirchengliedschaft. Kirchenschatz. Pluralismus. Praedestination. Privatoffenbarung. Propheten. Prophezeiung. Protestantismus. Protologie. Rechtfertigung. Religion.

(3) Karl Rahner, *On the Theology of Death,* New York, N.Y. (1961), quoted as *Th. of Death;* the same, Bemerkungen über das Naturgesetz und seine Erkennbarkeit: *Orientierung* 19 (1955), 239–243; quoted as: *Orientierung* 19 (1955); the same, Über das Verhältnis des Naturgesetzes zur übernatürlichen Gnadenordnung: *Orientierung* 20 (1956), 8–11; quoted as *Orientierung* 20 (1956); the same, Der Glaube des Priesters heute (a lecture delivered in 1962) after a typewritten copy of about twenty pages; quoted as: Gl.d.Pr.h.

Use was also made of the present book: Anita Röper, *Die Anonymen Christen,* quoted as: Röper.

[2] *Orientierung* 20 (1956) 11.

[3] Röper, p. ix.

[4] Zum Entwurf einer theologischen Anthropologie, cp. LThK I 618–627.

[5] Cp. II 82f. This concept of the people of God as mankind, united in the Incarnation and "consecrated" at least objectively, does not simply coincide with the use of the same word in the Bible.

[6] Cp. LThK I 623f.; LThK I 626f.

[7] Cp. V 15; V 387; LThK I 624; LThK IV 991f.; Gl.d.Pr.h. 13.

[8] Cp. V 208–212.

[9] Cp. LThK VIII 1169; H.d.W. 150–160: As shown by his receptive cognition, man is, even in his spiritual aspect, essentially related to matter. Because the spiritual soul itself is the formative principle of the body, it molds itself in his bodiliness.

[10] Cp. V 142; V 151f.; LThK VIII 1169.

[11] Cp. LThK IV 994; V 156; LThK VIII 1044.

[12] IV 137.

[13] Vatican I, sess.iii (Denz. 1794), referring to Is. 11, 12.

[14] Concerning the question of membership in the Church, we follow

the latest position of Rahner (LThK VI 223–225), which puts the ideas proposed previously in a new light. Cp. "Membership of the Church according to the Teaching of Pius XII's Encyclical 'Mystici Corporis Christi,'" II, 1–88 (esp. II, 26–34), where Rahner seems to hold to the position that there is only one kind of membership, imposing the invariable conditions of being baptized, professing the true faith and being united with the body of the Church.

15 LThK VI 223.

16 Cp. V 365.

17 Cp. LThK VI 223f.

18 Cp. LThK VI 224.

19 LThK VI 224.

17 Cp. LThK VI 223f.

18 Cp. LThK VI 224.

20 Cp. II 36f.

21 Cp. II 42f.; V 397; V 401. If even a finality towards the Church is necessary for salvation as a means, the faith implied in this finality is without doubt absolutely necessary as a means—or rather: it does not constitute an outward means for salvation, it is already in itself the beginning of salvation, hence indispensable for it.

22 Cp. V 144; II 45f.; II 59; II 83; V 397; LThK I 565; LThK VIII 1168.

23 Cp. V 387.

24 Cp. V 144f.; LThK IV 994; LThK VI 257.

25 V. 155.

26 Cp. II 47–50; II 76f.

27 Röper explains and discusses theories which differ from the one which follows, about the manner of reconciling God's universal salvific will with the necessity of faith as a means for salvation; cp. Röper, pp. 4ff., pp. 83–108.

28 Cp. LThK IV 991.

29 Cp. H.d. W. 111f.

30 Cp. I 84.

31 For this whole deduction, cp. LThK IV 992.

32 Even when the supernatural is offered to man, it remains a free gift, because "the sinner and unbeliever may refuse to accept this proffered self-manifestation of God without, in his very refusal, affirming that which he denies, as is the case of the sinful denial of his metaphysical essence" (LThK I 625). Thus writes Rahner, cp. also

Orientierung 19 (1955) 242, where it is shown that the pure, meta-physical nature of man, as contrasted with the supernatural and the whole historical situation of man, is posited by the inquiry about the conditions of the possibility of the spiritual act, especially the act of inquiring. Here Röper disagrees: "In this refusal he shows himself once more as the one who possesses this Christianity . . . we might say that the rejection of such transcendental necessities of one's nature occurs with that, or by virtue of that, which is rejected." (Röper p. 128.

[33] Gl.d.Pr.h. 17.

[34] Cp. I 311; and for a more detailed explanation H.d.W. 71–88: "As a spirit man knows things necessarily as beings; this is possible only if beyond every individual being the spirit reaches out towards being as such; as that which makes possible the knowledge of limitation as such, this being must be pure, infinite positivity, hence ultimately God himself. Therefore man is, on account of his spiritual nature, a being who stands open for God and thus for a possible revelation."

[35] Cp. IV 74f.; IV 69; IV 140f.; *Geist in Welt* 156–196: Man's spiritual power abstracts the form, and ultimately the being, from the individual thing represented by the senses. There is abstraction because the individual object is seen against the background of universal being, which encompasses in unity the fullness of reality. That is why the dynamism which enables man to abstract aims at the absolute being, at God, but in such a way that God is not grasped as "an object," since the dynamism which aims at him is precisely the condition of the possibility of any knowledge of objects. Frau Röper reaches the same conclusion by studying abstraction, the possibility of comparing, freedom, the principle of contradiction and the fact of inquiring.

[36] Cp. I,83f.; H.d.W. 117–134, 185–191: On the one hand God reveals himself, in the voluntary dynamism of freedom, as a free person who is not naturally accessible to the human mind in his own interiority, but who can freely manifest himself; on the other hand, on the basis of his unlimited horizon, man may accept, with his intellect, a free, historic communication from God, since words as carrying concepts which derive from the world through negation may transmit the knowledge of the supraterrestrial.

[37] Cp. IV 234.

[38] IV 214.

[39] I 185.

[40] IV 121.

[41] IV 149.

[42] Cp. IV 150.

[43] Cp. III 43f.

[44] LThK I 626.

[45] LThK I 626.

[46] Cp. I 28; I 163; V 20; V 21; V 212.

[47] Cp. I 186; IV 143.

[48] IV 140.

[49] Cp. I 186f.; III 39; III 42f.; IV 94; V 20–22.

[50] IV 141f.

[51] V 21f.

[52] Cp. V 199; V 201.

[53] Cp. IV 222.

[54] Cp. IV 122f.

[55] Cp. I 164f.

[56] Cp. V 207–212.

[57] I 164.

[58] Cp. V 205f.

[59] IV 148.

[60] Cp. III 43–45; IV 122f.; IV 148f.; LThK I 626.

[61] IV 149.

[62] I 186; cp. IV 143.

[63] Cp. I 309.

[64] Cp. IV 234.

[65] Cp. above, p. 151 and IV 143.

[66] Cp. IV 143.

[67] IV 234; IV 69; IV 74f. *Geist in Welt* 153–156 and 189–196: Man encounters the things of the world (and his fellow man) only in a spiritual-personal way, when he recognizes them as really self-subsistent and as beings; but the individual thing can be known as being only against the horizon of being as such—that is, of the absolute Being.

[68] Cp. I 186; I 315f.

[69] I 84; IV 149.

[70] Cp. H.d.W. 114f.

[71] IV 94.

72 Cp. I 302f.

73 Cp. I 375f.

74 Cp. I 312.

75 Cp. I 312; LThk VIII 1043.

76 Cp. I 313–316.

77 I 302; cp. I 311.

78 I 303.

79 Cp. LThk I 623.

80 Cp. II 239; IV 227; LThK I 565; Gl.d.Pr.h.17f.

81 Cp. LThK IV 992.

82 Cp. I 311f.

83 Cp. I 310; LThK IV 994.

84 Cp. v.g. I 335f.; IV 124f.; LThK VIII 800.

85 Cp. I 205; IV 54f.; LThK I 624; LThK IV 992; LThK IV 995; LThK VIII 800; LThK VIII 1044.

86 Cp. V. 144f.

87 Cp. IV 226f.

88 Cp. IV 54f.; LThK VIII 772; LThk VIII 800f.

89 Cp. I 362; II 79f.

90 From the point of view of terminology it is less equivocal and more useful to reserve, with Rahner (cp. V 155), the term "Christian" for those who have accepted their supernatural vocation explicitly or implicitly and anonymously. Because of the universal supernatural vocation Köper calls every human being a Christian (cp. Roger, pp. 126ff.), whether he has decided for or against the acceptance of Christianity.

91 Cp. I 361. *Geist in Welt* 236–242: Because man's spirit is a receptive spirit, man exercises the spirit's proper function of turning back upon itself every time he turns towards a datum of the senses.

92 I 362.

93 Cp. IV 142.

94 I 362.

95 V 16.

96 Cp. I 362f.; I 368; III 431.

97 Cp. V 116f.

98 IV 153.

99 Cp. I 376.

100 Cp. LThK IV 1001. *Geist in Welt* 81–84 and H.d.W. 54–62: The inquiry about being implies a previous knowledge of being; hence

being is already known, therefore also knowable, ordained towards knowledge. The mutual relation of being and knowing is metaphysically possible only if both are primordially one; that is, if by itself and according to its degree, being is knowable.

101 Cp. IV 230–232.

102 We overlook the built-in horizon of modern man produced by the history of Christianity; cp. LThK I 565.

103 IV 231.

104 Cp. v.g. IV 74f.; IV 77–80; IV 140f.; Gl.d.Pr.h. 14f.

105 Cp. IV 111.

106 Cp. *Geist in Welt* 189–192; IV 74f., IV 77.

107 Cp. III 429; LThK I 988.

108 Cp. LThK I 987.

109 History, cp. LThK IV 1001.

110 LThK IV 1001; cp. LThK VIII 1045.

111 Cp. LThK IV 1001.

112 Cp. IV 84; I 334f.

113 Cp. V 121–123.

114 Cp. I 377.

115 Cp. LThK IV 1001.

116 Cp. I 312; I 300; I 376f.; IV 225; IV 227f.; IV 230; LThK IV 1002.

117 Cp. LThK IV 1002.

118 Cp. I 378.

119 Gl.d.Pr.h. 12.

120 IV 54f.; cp. IV 84; V 154f.; V 397f.; V 405.

121 V 15. For further explanations about the way in which the Trinity, the Incarnation and Grace are experienced, cp. Röper, pp. 115–125.

122 Cp. IV 124f.; IV 128f.; V 15.

123 Cp. IV 144.

124 IV 144; cp. V 21; V 23.

125 V 16.

126 Gl.d.Pr.h. 13.

127 Cp. IV 153f.

128 Cp. V 15; V 154f.; V 123; V 397f.; V 405; IV 226–228; LThK IV 998.

129 Cp. *Th. of Death* 102–103; III 429.

130 Cp. V 122; IV 153f.

[131] IV 154.

[132] V 16.

[133] V 17.

[134] Concerning the problem of purely naturally good acts, cp. v.g. LThK IV 998; *Th. of Death* 96–104.

[135] Cp. V 404f.; I 35; *Th. of Death* 77–79; 94f.

[136] Cp. V 144f.; LThK IV 994; LThK VI 257; LThK VIII 801.

[137] IV 137.

[138] Cp. LThK IV 994; LThK VIII 1044.

[139] Cp. V 151f.

[140] Cp. LThK VI 224; V 389f.

[141] Cp. II 79f.

[142] I 287.

[143] Cp. II 197.

[144] Cp. II 124. *Geist in Welt* 294–300: The spiritual powers emanate from the soul before the sense powers and as their origin, so that their spiritual activities may take shape in and through the senses which stand against them.

[145] Cp. LThK IV 994.

[146] Cp. II 85–87; V 397; LThK VI 224.

[147] II 87.

[148] Cp. LThK VI 225.

[149] Cp. II 87.

[150] Cp. II 85.

[151] Cp. V 17f.; V 143; LThK V 75; LThK VIII 801; LThK VIII 1168f.

[152] Cp. V 17.

[153] Cp. V 404; IV 153f.; V 154f.

[154] Cp. V 400f.; V 402; V 406; V 156.

[155] Cp. V 378.

[156] Cp. V 156; V 365; LThK VIII 1044.

[157] Cp. III 437; IV 228f.; V 158; Gl.d.Pr.h. 19.